EMPOWERED
TO PRAY

Books by Woodrow Kroll

Early in the Morning
Tested by Fire
The Vanishing Ministry
Bible Country
Prodigal People
Is There a Man in the House?
The Twelve Voices of Christmas
The Twelve Voices of Easter

EMPOWERED
TO PRAY

*Ten Great Prayers of the Bible
Reveal the Secrets of
Praying with Power*

WOODROW KROLL

Baker Books

A Division of Baker Book House Co
Grand Rapids, Michigan 49516

Published by Baker Books
a division of Baker Book House Company
P.O. Box 6287, Grand Rapids, MI 49516-6287

Printed in the United States of America

Library of Congress Cataloging-in-Publication Data

Kroll, Woodrow Michael, 1944-
    Empowered to pray : ten great prayers of the Bible reveal the secrets of praying with power / Woodrow Kroll.
       p.   cm.
    ISBN 0-8010-5233-5
      1. Bible—Prayers. 2. Bible—Prayers—History and criticism. 3. Prayer. I. Title.
BS680.P64K76   1995
242'.722—dc20   95-32357

Dedicated
to
the prayer partners of
Back to the Bible
and to
Matilda Epp
Betty Wiersbe
and
Linda Kroll
who have spent much
time on their knees
to keep their husbands
on the air

Contents

Contents

Preface

Life was so much simpler when I was a boy. Television was just becoming popular. Howdy Doody, the Lone Ranger, and Captain Video were my heroes. There were choices to make and chores to do. In those days the chores presented more challenges than the choices.

But T.V., chores, or choices did not alter the one constant in our lives. We attended church faithfully. We were there on Sunday morning, both for Sunday school and church. We were back Sunday night for the youth meeting and evening service. We were there on Wednesday night for prayer meeting. Our church habits were never challenged and therefore never changed.

But during those years some of the values we cherished were challenged and changed. Prayer, for example. Praying to God was so much a part of life back then that we even prayed in school. I read the Bible and led my homeroom in prayer every day during my senior year in high school. But in 1963 the United States Supreme Court banned prayer and Bible reading from public schools. The impact of prayer on our nation's soul waned dramatically.

Sure, there were pockets of resistance. A sign in a Nebraska high school read "In case of a tornado, the Supreme Court ruling against prayer in school will be temporarily suspended." But the resistance was more tongue-in-cheek than empowered. The impact of prayer on the average person has never been the same.

But in the last decade there has been a resurgence of interest in prayer. Perhaps the mess we're in politically, ethically, morally, spiritually, and financially has driven us to our knees. It certainly should. For whatever reasons, God's people are experiencing a renewal of prayer awareness.

In the American Northwest a group of men and women have been praying for world revival. Where I live, several dozen pastors and I have been praying that revival would grip our city. David Bryant has had a significant ministry with his Concerts of Prayer. J. Gordon Henry, an educator and pastor, was so changed by discovering the power of prayer that he dedicated his life to conducting prayer seminars. Story after story surfaces about pockets of prayer changing the face of the church.

Writing in *Christianity Today* (Aug. 16, 1993), Kenneth Kantzer described the explosion of the church in Korea, which is fast becoming a center for world evangelism. Kantzer asked a well-known Korean pastor why he thought the Korean church had flourished so dramatically in the last fifty years.

The pastor put his chin in his hand thoughtfully and did not answer for several minutes. Then he said, "I think it is because we lived under severe Japanese persecution for so long. We learned to have no hope in ourselves, but only in God. And we learned to pray. We have been a suffering church and, therefore, a praying church."

Prayer is the preface to real purpose, the prologue to God's power, the prelude to personal peace, and the precursor to world evangelism. When the ministry of prayer is elevated, so is every other ministry. Preaching becomes better with prayer. Witnessing becomes more effective with prayer. Government becomes more just with prayer.

But if prayer is so vital, why don't we do it more often? If it's so important, why don't we do it better? Why do we grope for answers about how to pray, when to pray, what to pray for? Are we only paying lip service to the importance of prayer?

Prayer is a gift from God. It's the one gift all Christians can enjoy equally. Praying for one another is the believer's privilege because our access to God was paid for by the blood of his Son. (Read Romans 5:1–2 and Ephesians 2:18.) Without the gift of God's Son, we would have no access to God. But this book is not about prayer as God's gift.

Prayer is a cry from the heart. Time and again the psalmist cried out to God in prayer. He hungered to be near God, to enjoy conversation with God. (Read Psalms 27:8; 42:1; 84:2; 119:2, 45.) Rarely do we pray well unless we have this same longing thirst for God. Prayer quenches that thirst, but this book is not about prayer as a cry from the heart.

Prayer is a work of the Holy Spirit. When we pray effectively, we use a divine lubricant—the Holy Spirit. He makes sure our prayers are accurately communicated to God. Because we are God's children, the Holy Spirit cries to God in our behalf (Gal. 4:6) and even makes intercession for us (Rom. 8:26–27). But this book is not about the work of the Holy Spirit in prayer.

Prayer is a skill developed. When we pray effectively one time, it helps us pray more effectively the next. Listen to others who pray effectively and learn about the skill of prayer. Some people just seem to pray better than others, but it has nothing to do with their vocabulary. Why is that? What are the keys to developing skill in prayer? That's what this book is about.

We hear a lot of talk about empowerment these days. This book is about empowerment, about being empowered to pray. It's an intimate look at some of the great prayers of the Bible. It's an insider's view of what pleases God when we pray—the insiders being biblical characters who knew how to pray.

This is not a book recounting amazing answers to prayer. It is not a theological discussion of the basis of our access to God. It is not a plea for more heartfelt prayers or more Spirit-filled prayers. All of these are found elsewhere. This is a book that examines the skillful prayers of biblical characters.

When the Hellenistic widows were being neglected and the Jerusalem church selected deacons to look after their needs, the apostles gave themselves wholly to prayer and the ministry of the Word (Acts 6:4). They elevated the ministry of prayer to the same position of importance as the ministry of preaching. If we spend time developing our skills to preach to men, isn't it reasonable to develop our skills to pray to God? That's what this book is about.

I have grouped ten great prayers of the Bible into three sections. The first four chapters teach us about preparing to pray. These prayers demonstrate the skill of gathering sufficient facts to pray intelligently. They show how to come to God in the right attitude, with clean hands and a pure heart. God's answers have the uncanny habit of favoring those who have paid the price of preparation.

The middle chapters zero in on what we should pray for. This requires some acquired skill as well. We must learn to ask for things that are in harmony with the character and will of God. Often we come to God with a long shopping list. But does our list reflect God's agenda or our agenda? Are we just trying to get God to sign off on our interests, or do our prayers also reflect his interests? And when we bring our concerns to God, do we underestimate the need? Do we nickel-and-dime God when there are major needs in our life?

Chapters eight, nine, and ten reflect the request of Jesus' disciples to be taught how to pray. His disciples still request this. Although a pattern for prayer is seen in most of the great prayers of the Bible, these chapters specifically address what's important and what's not important in being empowered to pray. These are the *how* chapters on prayer.

When God sacrificed his Son at Calvary, he not only secured our eternal destiny, he restored the heavenly fiber-optic system we call prayer. Empowerment to pray has as much to do with praying skillfully as anything. Those who prayed skillfully in the Bible were not all heroes. They were not all religious leaders. They were not all celebrities. But they were all empowered to pray.

A renewal of interest in prayer is not enough. It must be accompanied by understanding what empowers us to pray and the development of the skills that make prayer powerful. It's one thing to attend a prayer meeting; it's quite another to go away forever changed.

Perhaps Charles G. Finney was right. He said, "I am convinced that nothing in Christianity is so rarely attained as a praying heart." Finney was not simply talking about tenderness but about skill, the skill of praying with power.

I've addressed both the head and the heart in this book. The great prayers of the Bible reflect people who really knew how to pray. Their prayers show signs of preparation and thought. But they also reflect warmth of heart. Great prayers are an explosive mix of passion and preparation, knowing what to pray for and how to pray.

If this book eases the path to God's throne room and excites you about the joys of empowered prayer, then my prayers will have been answered.

Part 1

PREPARING TO PRAY

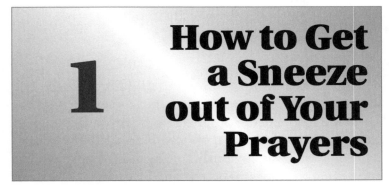

1 How to Get a Sneeze out of Your Prayers

Elisha's Prayer
2 Kings 4:8–37

Being empowered to pray means gathering enough information before you pray that you are not embarrassingly ignorant when you pray.

A h-choo!"

"Gesundheit."

"Thank you."

Have you noticed the cycle of comments that often complete a sneeze? Prayer is like that. It isn't finished until you hear something.

When we pray, we want God to hear us, and we want him to answer. We don't pray just because we like to; we

17

pray for results. Do you know how to get a sneeze out of your prayers? Do you know how to get answers? Grab a tissue and let's learn from a man who did.

The great prayers of the Bible share many characteristics. One is effective preparation. Getting ready to pray is a key ingredient in being empowered to pray. If you don't get results from your prayers, maybe you haven't spent enough time getting ready to pray.

AN EMPOWERED PROPHET

Elisha was a ninth century B.C. prophet in Israel. His ministry was punctuated with miracle after miracle. He saved the school of the prophets from certain death when they got hold of a bad pot of stew. He healed Naaman of leprosy. Elisha was obviously an empowered prophet. No story demonstrates this better than his raising a boy from the dead. In 2 Kings 4:8–37 we see how to get a sneeze out of our prayers.

Elisha frequently traveled from his Mount Carmel retreat to the cities of Galilee. On the way he passed through the little village of Shunem where he befriended a wealthy but childless couple. He regularly stopped by for a visit and was entertained by his Shunammite friends.

The wife knew Elisha was a man of God. She proposed they build a rooftop room for him. It was small and spartanly furnished—just a bed, table, chair, and lamp.

Elisha was pleased with his guest chamber and wanted to return the couple's kindness. He announced that the following year about that time God would give them a child. The Shunammite woman was incredulous, but a year later she gave birth to a son.

At age five or six the little guy tagged along with his father to the field. But the Palestinian sun was hot, and the boy suffered from sunstroke. Sunstroke was common in Israel, and the father knew exactly what to do. He sent the boy into the shade of the house and the love of his mother.

The Shunammite woman nursed the boy until noon, but to no avail. He died. She carried her lifeless son upstairs and laid him on Elisha's bed. She called to her husband for a servant and a donkey to make a hurried trip to see Elisha at Mount Carmel. With her child dead, the Shunammite's haste was understandable. When she arrived at Mount Carmel, Elisha spotted her a great distance away. He told his servant Gehazi, "Run to meet her and ask her, 'Are you all right? Is your husband all right? Is your child all right?'" (v. 26).

That wasn't just idle chitchat. Elisha had no idea why the woman was coming to him, and he needed information to be of help. The Shunammite had captured his full attention.

The woman wanted Elisha to do something, anything. All Elisha could do was pray. The situation was desperate. Would he rush to prayer? No! Empowered prayer requires preparation. Elisha wanted information before he prayed.

Your pastor stands behind the pulpit. It's time to preach. He opens his mouth and out come a few random thoughts that just popped into his head. He hasn't prepared anything. He says, "This morning I'm just going to share with you." Don't expect much.

If your pastor never prepared his messages, how seriously would you take his sermons? If his habit was to "wing it" week after week, you'd want to form a pulpit committee and begin considering a replacement.

Don't we do the same thing with God? We stand before him, without having gathered the facts, and say whatever comes to mind. We wing it time after time. How long do we expect God to listen to such prayers? How long *should* he listen?

Preparing to pray makes the same good sense that preparing to preach does. Unless your situation demands instant prayer, don't just rush into prayer. That robs you of power, for power and preparation go hand in hand.

How to Get Ready to Pray

It's important that your prayers be both informed and intelligent. Elisha gathered as much information as he could before he prayed. He was completely focused on the Shunammite woman and her need. Are you focused when you pray? Do you concentrate on one item of prayer at a time? Do you know enough about your request to focus God's attention on it?

Perhaps Elisha can help. Here are the four steps he took in getting the facts that empowered him to pray.

Focus on Specifics

Elisha was at his mountain retreat. He needed some rest and relaxation, but when the Shunammite woman approached, he focused solely on her and her need. He said, "Look! There's the Shunammite!"

If you feel your prayers are powerless, perhaps they would be more effective if you were more specific and focused when talking with God. Instead of saying, "Look, Lord! There's a whole world that needs you," try saying, "Look! There's the Shunammite!"

In cameras with automatic focus you can push a button to bring the subject into sharper focus. Maybe you should do that with your prayers.

As you give thanks before the evening meal, if your children are waiting to dig in, if the aroma of pizza is wafting past their little noses and prompting a symphony of growls in their stomachs, you wouldn't begin praying alphabetically for the missionaries—from Afghanistan to Zaire. If you did, you'd have a justifiable mutiny on your hands.

Be focused when you pray. Blot from your mind everything unimportant at the time. Prepare for prayer by zeroing in on what you want to talk with God about. One time you may say, "Look! There's the Shunammite!" and another time, "It's me, it's me, it's me, O Lord, standin' in the need of prayer."

Visualize the Request

When Elisha spotted the Shunammite, she wasn't alone. There was a servant with her, leading the donkey. Elisha must have noticed the man and beast, but he "saw" only the woman.

In preparing yourself to pray for someone, visualize that person in your mind. I'm not referring to the New Age technique of visualization but simply to picturing a face in your mind. This helps to personalize your prayer, and it helps to make the person and his or her need more real.

Each night my family and I have a quiet time with the Lord. After we read and discuss the Word, we pray as a family. Years ago we hit on a great idea. Each year at Christmas we receive many cards from friends and family. We used to read them, enjoy memories of the sender, and then throw the cards away. Not anymore. Now we keep our Christmas cards in a basket along with prayer cards from missionary friends. Each night we choose a card and pray for the sender. That way we enjoy their Christmas greetings all year long, and they enjoy the benefits of our prayers all year long.

Taking our cue from Elisha, we see the faces of our friends before we close our eyes to pray, which makes them very real to us as we intercede for them. Visualizing your request helps you be more intimate in prayer. It helps you pray with your heart, not just with your lips. Elisha was still a long way from praying for the woman's son, but already he was getting the picture.

Gather Useful Information

When Elisha inquired if the Shunammite, her husband, and her child were all right, he was doing more than just being polite. Her responses would tell him if one of them had a need for which he should pray. He was gathering data. We should do the same.

In our information age we're suffering from an information glut. We receive more junk mail, see more things on T.V., read more things in the newspaper than we can digest or profitably use. Yet when we pray, we often suffer from a lack of information.

Prepare intelligently; pray intelligently. Forage for facts. Ask questions. Identify specific needs. Keep from praying in generalities. Rule out the things you don't need to pray for at this time.

I once preached in Jamaica, holding radio rallies all over the island. While in Kingston I had a private meeting with the governor general. Before I met him, I inquired about protocol. What should I call him? What sort of man was he? I was delighted to learn he was a fine

Christian, but I didn't want to have an audience with the governor general without getting my facts straight first.

Sometimes our prayers are so hastily conceived we don't have our facts right. Do we offend God's intelligence? Maybe so. We pray about things of which we are ill-informed or uninformed. Our inadequate preparation for prayer must speak volumes to God!

You can avoid that as Elisha did. Ask questions. Get the facts before you pray.

Here's a final step Elisha took in gathering information.

Recognize the Emotional State of Those Requesting Prayer

Have you ever prayed for someone you knew was at the end of his rope? One day I received a phone call from a frantic woman. She was determined to talk with me; no one else would do. She sounded so desperate my secretary put the call through. For the first few minutes I heard nothing but sobs. She couldn't manage a word. I waited with an occasional word of encouragement. After calming down, she tearfully told me her story.

She was at the end of her rope. A former vice president of a large company, this distraught woman was out of work, out of friends, and out of hope. She had decided to take her own life and for whatever reason chose me to be the last person she would talk with. After talking and praying with her, I made some calls to get additional help for her. Things turned around in her life. God still heals the emotions and helps the hurting heart.

When preparing to pray for someone, it's helpful to be discerning about his or her emotional state. Sizing up the heart and mind is another way of getting prepared before you pray.

When the Shunammite woman reached Elisha, she knelt down and grabbed his feet. Apparently Gehazi did not understand the woman's intent and tried to push her away. But Elisha looked more deeply into her soul than did his servant. He said, "Leave her alone! She is in bitter distress" (v. 27).

The Bible does not say the woman told Elisha her child was dead. Preparing to pray for someone requires that we hear that person's heart, not just his or her request. Many times missionaries have sent reports to their supporting churches that mask their real prayer needs. Sometimes our children have said everything is okay when they didn't mean it at all. We need to be sensitive to more than the words to know what people are really saying.

If you want to pray well, pray wisely. Focus on specifics in your preparation. Visualize those you're praying for. Gather useful information about your request. Remember, sometimes you have to see the real request in a person's face because you won't hear it in his or her voice.

Elisha did all this in preparation for prayer. As you can see, preparation does not always require a lot of time but it does require focus and concentration. Fix your heart and mind on someone in particular when you prepare to pray and see if you are not empowered as Elisha was.

One other thing. As you will see later in this book, specifically in the prayer of Hezekiah, you will not always have time for significant reflection before you pray. God looks on the heart and discerns your prayer attitude. He honors appropriate attitudes in times of emergency. But if time for preparation is available, we must take the time to prepare adequately. It's how we're empowered to pray.

GET SERIOUS WHEN YOU PRAY

Preparation is not prayer. The troubled woman fell at Elisha's feet. She poured out her heart about her son. It was time for action. Elisha told Gehazi to run to the woman's house, go to the prophet's chamber, and attend to the boy. Gehazi was to take Elisha's staff, place it on the boy's face, and see what happened. That's pretty weird.

Elisha was not looking for magic, but in the Bible God sometimes performed miracles in strange ways. Remember the woman who touched the hem of Jesus' garment and was healed (Mark 5:25–34)? Or when handkerchiefs and aprons that touched Paul were used to heal the sick and cast out evil spirits (Acts 19:12)? These certainly were remarkable.

But these were unusual events—exceptions, not the rule. "Is any one of you sick? He should call the elders of the church to pray over him and anoint him with oil in the name of the Lord" (James 5:14). That's the biblical pattern, not staffs or prayer cloths or other paraphernalia.

When the staff solution proved unsuccessful, Gehazi returned to Elisha. The prophet and the woman were already on their way to Shunem. Prayer was the only answer.

Waste No Time

The prophet got right down to business. "When Elisha reached the house, there was the boy lying dead on his couch. He went in, shut the door on the two of them and prayed to the Lord" (vv. 32–33). Prayer was the only solution and there was no sense in waiting.

That's a good lesson for us. We can try a dozen remedies, but sometimes only prayer holds the solution. Get the facts and then get right to prayer. After all, if God alone has the power, and prayer alone has the key to unlock that power, what are we waiting for?

The prophet was not praying for the sick to recover; he was praying for the dead to rise. That was a tall order. God chose not to perform a miracle with the staff. Would he choose to perform a miracle without it? Would God answer Elisha's prayer? What if he didn't? Would that destroy the prophet's credibility? Elisha would risk everything on a prayer.

Pray Alone

Arriving at the woman's house, Elisha hurried to his chamber. He closed the door behind him so no one could disturb him.

I like to pray with others. Praying with family or friends is a privilege. But there are times when praying is best done alone. Again and again the great prayers of the Bible reveal the power of intercessory solitude. Didn't Jesus go off by himself and pray alone in the Garden of Gethsemane? There's something about getting alone with God that makes your prayer more intimate and personal. You can cut through all the prayer clichés and say exactly what you mean.

Are you facing a serious situation today? If so, it's good to ask others to pray for you. Pray with them about your situation. But God also empowers you to pray by yourself. If you've never experienced the intercessory solitude that Elisha did, try it. Shut the door. Shut out everybody else. Get alone with God. Speak with him as if he were the only other person in the room. He is!

Make Contact

For the most part, Westerners are not a touchy people. We like to keep our distance. We'll shake hands, maybe even give an occasional hug, but that's about it. The ancient Near East was much different. When you greeted someone, it meant a hug and kiss on each cheek. Even today it's not uncommon to see men walking arm in arm down the streets in the Old City of Jerusalem.

When Elisha shut everyone out of the room, he laid his body over the dead boy—eyes to eyes, mouth to mouth, hands to hands. It wasn't a perfect fit; this was a boy, and Elisha was a man.

What was he trying to do? Was the prophet administering mouth-to-mouth resuscitation? Some people have thought so, but the boy was dead. Even mouth-to-mouth won't raise the dead. Perhaps he was just mimicking his mentor, Elijah, who years before raised a widow's son from the dead by doing the same thing (1 Kings 17:21). Though we can't fully explain the prophets' actions, we can learn from them. Both Elisha and Elijah did more than sit by while they prayed. They actively involved themselves with those for whom they prayed.

Have you ever had someone put his arm around you while he prayed for you? Perhaps he held your hand. Maybe you have joined hands in a circle to pray. I have held my children when they were little babies and prayed for them when they were sick. They've climbed up on my knee as toddlers, and I've prayed for them. I've held their hands when they left for college and prayed for them. Somehow the serious business of prayer seems more serious when you make contact with the one you're praying for.

The next time you join someone in prayer, "join" them in prayer. Be discreet, of course, but don't worry about what people will say. We've all seen football players who join hands in the huddle, and they don't worry about what people say. Why should we?

Making contact is much more than laying hands on the sick. It's joining heart to heart, hand to hand, and agreeing with each other in prayer (Matt. 18:19). Try it. You may be surprised at the power you're missing.

Repeat Your Prayers

When you pull up to the drive-thru to order a burger or some hot wings, usually a cheery voice will say, "Thank you. Come again." They know you'll be back. Why? Because one trip to the restaurant is never enough. That burger will soon be gone and you'll be hungry again. Eating must be repeated. Your hunger lets you know that once is not enough.

Prayer is not a once-and-forget-it thing either. God delights in hearing your voice; he never tires of it. God never rebukes us for coming to him too often. He never upbraids us, never reproaches us (James 1:5). He never says, "Oh no, not you again." He wants us to return to him in prayer time after time.

Every person who is successful at prayer has learned you don't pray and forget about it. You pray and pray again. Three times Elijah stretched himself on the widow's son when he prayed; twice his pupil did the same. Empowerment is enhanced by repetition. Take a tip from Elisha's repeated prayer. Don't stop with one trip to God's pray-thru window. He is looking for repeat visits.

Pray and Walk; Walk and Pray

When Elisha stretched himself on the boy, immediately the boy's cold body began to warm. I'm not a medical doctor, so I can't explain this. Maybe doctors can't either. But that's what 2 Kings 4:34 says. The lifeless body took warmth from Elisha's body, but it did not revive.

Elisha's staff had failed, and now it appeared his prayer had failed as well. He created a little heat but no life.

Could nothing more be done? Would he give up? Would he have the courage to face the woman and tell her it was all over? Would he admit failure and go back to Carmel?

No, he wouldn't give up, and neither should you if your prayers aren't answered the first time. Do what Elisha did. Verse 35 says he turned away from the boy's body and walked back and forth in the room. The prophet took a break from praying on his face and began praying on his feet. Prayer in motion!

I like to do things standing up. I do much of my thinking and planning while I walk. I pace and think, pace and think. Sometimes I just pace, but eventually thoughts come. Some of my greatest times in prayer have been while I was on my feet.

Although we usually sit down to pray, if the answer does not come quickly, or the situation does not appear to change, try getting up and walking around. Change your position, but don't change your prayer. Elisha took a break from the boy, but he continued to commune with God.

Go Back to Prayer

Having paced the room, Elisha returned to the bed. Again he stretched himself on the boy and fervently prayed. Prayer is not finished until there is a response. Phillips Brooks said, "Prayer is not conquering God's reluctance, but taking hold of God's willingness." Elisha didn't return to prayer to wear God down; you can't wear God down. He returned to prayer to take hold of God's willingness, and it worked.

God's response to the prophet's second round of praying was much different from the first. This time the boy sneezed seven times and opened his eyes.

Don't miss this!

The boy died of sunstroke. He couldn't take a breath. He couldn't make a sound. There was no air in his lungs. He was dead. But he sneezed. And then he sneezed again. And then two more times. And then three more times. Seven sneezes from breathless lungs!

Do you know what a sneeze is? Webster says to sneeze is "to exhale breath from the nose and mouth in a sudden, involuntary, explosive action." You've exploded into a sneeze many times. You know a great deal of air is expelled when you do. But this boy was dead. He hadn't taken a breath in a long time. Still, God gave him breath and he sneezed and sneezed and sneezed. It was a miracle of God brought about by prayer.

Elisha got a sneeze out of his prayer. In fact, he got seven sneezes. What do you get out of your prayers? If you want to get a sneeze out of your prayers, do what the prophet did. Get the facts before you pray. Get serious when you pray. And get used to repeating prayer.

ON-LINE PRAYER

What does it mean to be empowered to pray? It means gathering enough information before you pray that you are not embarrassingly ignorant when you pray.

Get your facts straight. Praying with power means you've done your homework. Preparation is not always possible when we pray, but it's not always impossible. In fact, we are more likely to have time to prepare for prayer than not—unless our prayer lives are so shoddy we always pray on the spur of the moment. When we take time to get the facts—names, places, specifics—we pray more intelligently, and then we are empowered by the Holy Spirit to pray.

Our Father, the God who brings light to darkness, the God who brings life out of death, to you, O God, we bring our prayer. Impress us with the needs around us. Impress us with our responsibility to gather the facts in preparation to pray. And once we are ready, Lord, empower us to pray by your Spirit. Help us to get right to it and stay with it. As we respond to needs, please respond to our prayers. Prepare us to speak with you. Reward our preparation with your response. Like Elisha, help us to get a sneeze out of our prayers. In the name of Jesus. Amen.

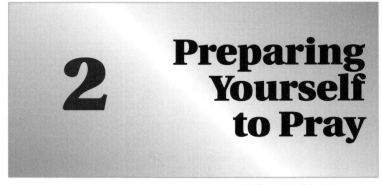

Preparing Yourself to Pray

2

Nehemiah's Prayer
Nehemiah 1:1–11

Being empowered to pray means taking the right steps to prepare yourself for a serious conversation with God.

Being empowered to pray begins with having the facts at hand before you approach God. But facts are just facts; they aren't the only kind of preparation that brings power. Personal preparation is also at the heart of having power with God.

When someone says to you, "Have a good day," how do you respond? If you're like I am, you probably say something meaningless like "Thanks. You too." We say that so glibly the words have little meaning. It's like a smiley face—all sentiment and no substance.

But we don't always have a good day, do we? We'd like each day to be a good one, but it doesn't work out that way. From eternity's point of view, it's more important that we have a godly day than a good one. After all, you can have a godly day even if you don't have a good day, but you can never really have a good day if it isn't also a godly day.

If you've ever heard me on the radio, you know I close every *Back to the Bible* broadcast with the same words. They've become my signature closing. "Have a good and godly day."

One of the keys to having a good and godly day is paying attention to details. We wander from godliness not so much by becoming adulterous or idolatrous but simply by forgetting the things that please the Lord. When our daily quiet time with the Lord lapses, our prayer life begins to suffer. Soon we miss some services at church, and then we begin to plan weekend events that make going to church impossible.

Would you like it if someone said you were pious? Probably not. Most people confuse being pious with being pompous. But piety is an attitude of wanting to please God in all things. It's godly behavior, especially in an ungodly environment.

Nehemiah was a godly man in an ungodly world. He was pious. He must have had many days that were not good ones, but he tried to make every day a godly one. That's what makes him stand out—a pious person in an impious empire.

The Book of Nehemiah is a diary, the running commentary of a pious man's daily activities. Nehemiah begins his diary with a prayer, one of the great prayers of the Bible. By reading it you'll learn something about intimacy with God, about piety, about godliness, and in the process something about being empowered to pray.

PIETY AND PERSONALITY

Piety is not so much what you do but who you are. You may describe someone by saying, "There goes a godly person," but what do you mean by that? Down deep inside you probably know that person means what he says and believes in what he does. But how do you know for sure? There is no better way to uncover true piety than by hearing someone pray. Then watch that person. Does he or she have pedestrian piety, piety with feet? If so, that person is a godly person.

During the dark years of the Babylonian captivity, God raised up champions among the Jewish people. These were men and women of piety, people who were godly down deep inside, and their lives reflected it. These were not shallow people with fragile spiritual psyches. They were giants, people who had their spiritual acts together. One of those giants was Nehemiah.

Years before Nehemiah's birth the Babylonians destroyed Jerusalem's houses, walls, even its famous temple. These eastern invaders carried the Jews into exile where they remained for seventy years (Jer. 25:1, 11–12). But the power of the Babylonian empire was broken on October 19, 539 B.C. The Persian king Cyrus liberated all expatriates and decreed that every captive should return to his homeland. This initiated several waves of Jewish emigration to the Holy Land.

In 538 B.C. the first group of Jews returned under the leadership of Zerubbabel (Ezra 1:1–2:2). They met significant opposition from the Samaritans but succeeded in rebuilding the temple in 515 B.C.

A second group returned in 458 B.C. led by Ezra (Ezra 7:1–10). He found the Jews were not piously attending to the will of God. In fact, they were in significant moral decline. But Ezra's faithful teaching ministry turned many back to God.

About 444 B.C. a third wave of emigration occurred under the leadership of Nehemiah. What he accomplished in a short time is amazing. God used him to oversee the rebuilding of Jerusalem's walls and bring the Jews to greater commitment in keeping God's Law.

PIETY IN THE PALACE

Nehemiah's diary gives us a glimpse inside the royal palace of ancient Persia. King Artaxerxes truly had the lifestyle of the rich and famous. Nehemiah was serving the Persian king in his winter palace at Susa or Shushan (Esther 1:2; Dan. 8:2). He was the king's personal cupbearer.

Being a cupbearer must have had its moments. The cupbearer would taste the king's wine before serving it, insuring it had not been poisoned. Obviously cupbearers were expendable. But the position had its up side too. The king trusted Nehemiah. Nehemiah was more than a cupbearer; he was the king's confidant and friend.

It would be a mistake, however, to think Nehemiah abandoned his piety to facilitate his meteoric rise in power circles. He didn't. Nehemiah brought his piety to work with him. He did what his job called for, but he did it without forgetting his God, his people, or his homeland. They were never far from his mind or, when the opportunity presented itself, from his lips. Nehemiah's days may not always have been good ones, but you can be sure they always were godly ones.

Others have come to positions of prominence in their government without abandoning their piety. William E. Gladstone was a devout Christian, an earnest student of the Bible, and a man of prayer. His moral values directed his sixty-two years in British political life as a member of parliament, three times chancellor of the exchequer, and four times prime minister.

Abraham Kuyper is best known as a Dutch theologian, but he did not abandon his biblical beliefs when he became a member of the States-General and later prime minister of the Netherlands.

More recently, Senator Dan Quayle became vice president of the United States. When he brought his Christian values, especially family values, from Indiana to Washington, D.C., he was hooted on Capitol Hill. But piety should be at home in the palace. We could only wish it were more at home in some of our palaces today.

PIETY AND PATRIOTISM

News from home is always welcome. In the month of Kislev, roughly corresponding to our December, word came to Nehemiah that Hanani and some other men had just returned from Judah. Nehemiah was anxious to hear how things were going with Ezra and those who had returned to Judah a dozen years earlier.

Unfortunately the news was mostly bad. Much of Ezra's work was spiritual not physical. Jerusalem was still in shambles. The city wall had huge gaping holes in it. Brigands and armed thugs could ride into the city and rob the people at will.

It's here that Nehemiah's diary betrays his godly character. Nehemiah knew it was time for prayer. Prayer works best when nothing else works at all! When the situation appears hopeless, prayer fosters hope. The news from Jerusalem did not drive Nehemiah to despair. Instead, it drove him to his knees. That's where bad news should always drive us. There's no power like prayer power. Prayer shouldn't be our last resort; it should be our first thought.

Before Nehemiah prayed, however, he prepared himself to pray. He had learned one of the secrets of being empowered to pray. He got himself into a prayer posture. I don't mean he got down on his knees. Posture means much more than physical position. Among other things, the noun means "a conscious mental or outward behavioral attitude."

That's our focus in this chapter—our posture in prayer. How do we get our minds and hearts ready to pray? It's easy to gather data, and it's easy to assume a physical position. But it's our hearts and minds that need the most preparation for prayer.

PIETY AND PREPARATION

Some people require high maintenance. Maybe you're married to one. They need things done for them all the time. They need their food cooked, houses kept clean, clothes ironed. They don't know what any of the settings on the washing machine are for. They need constant attention.

Nehemiah was a busy man who served a thirsty king. Artaxerxes was one of the most powerful men in the world, and with power came constant demands. King Artaxerxes was a high-maintenance person. He needed frequent attention, and that was Nehemiah's job.

But there was news from Jerusalem, and it was bad news. Nehemiah wrote in his diary, "When I heard these things,

I sat down and wept. For some days I mourned and fasted and prayed before the God of heaven" (Neh. 1:4).

We can learn as much about being empowered to pray by Nehemiah's personal preparation as we can by his prayer. The verbs in this verse tell us a great deal about Nehemiah's posture before prayer. Notice the components of his preparation and how often we forget them.

Nehemiah Stopped All Activity

Nehemiah temporarily thought little about the king. His thoughts were consumed with Jerusalem. Nehemiah was a man of action, but first he was a man of prayer.

Jerusalem's distress required prayer, but prayer born out of stillness, not activity. Nehemiah would have to stop and pray. Could he shoot a prayer up to God while he buzzed around the palace in his daily routine? Certainly, but that wouldn't do.

We've all had occasions to pray on the run, and there's nothing wrong with that. In the last chapter I spoke of walking around while praying. But the most thoughtful prayer comes when we do nothing else, when we stop and let the world rush on. Great prayers come from the crucible of inactive silence.

If you want to be empowered to pray, put other things aside when you pray. Tune everything else out of your life. That's the way to posture yourself to pray with power. It quiets your heart and heightens your awareness of the presence of God. Take a prayer break and seek the guidance of the Holy Spirit.

Time out for God is never ill spent. Jesus took time out in the Garden of Gethsemane. That was a busy night for him, but his time in prayer kept him on course to

Calvary. It's when we are busiest for God that we need to take additional time out to posture for prayer.

Jim is an on-the-go executive, the chief operating officer of a multimillion dollar corporation. But in all the years I've known him, I've never seen him too busy to pray. He lives in the country and attends a tiny community church. Still, Jim meets weekly in his office over a brown-bag lunch with the other elders of his church. They pray for their pastor and church needs. He postures himself for prayer by taking time out of a busy day.

Too often we posture ourselves for prayer only when we're at the end of our rope. When we reach the most dire circumstances, that's when we take time out to gear up for prayer. At the death of a loved one, at the news of a tragic automobile accident, that's when we're willing to stop and pray. But stopping often to seek God's guidance is something we all need to do daily. That's one way we are empowered, by setting aside all activity and sitting still before God.

Is God saying to you, "Take a seat. Let's talk"? If so, posture your heart and mind for prayer. Do what it takes to be empowered to pray. Pull over, stand still, hang up, hit the off button, do whatever is necessary to take a seat and talk with God. "Be still, and know that I am God" (Ps. 46:10). It may be the most valuable time of your day.

Nehemiah Wept

Nehemiah slowed down by sitting down. That was a start, but it wasn't enough. Nehemiah took his seat to alter his routine and prepare his heart for prayer, but there are other components to his personal preparation for prayer. Weeping was one of them.

Nehemiah writes, "When I heard these things, I sat down and wept" (1:4). When Nehemiah said he wept, he didn't just mean he felt lousy. The word he used (Hebrew, *bakah*) means to drop or to flow in drops. It's the same word used of Joseph's tears when he revealed himself to his brothers (Gen. 45:14). It indicates both a heightened level of sadness and a deepened need for prayer. Perhaps you have experienced the pain of a runaway son or daughter. You have shed countless tears in the weeks or months they have been gone. Weeping is a wonderful emotional release, but by itself it won't bring your teenager back.

Praying is a better option. It is still one of our most empowered weapons against Satan. Prayer should never be taken lightly. Empowered prayer sends shudders up Satan's spine. And when prayer is well watered with tears, that really must make Satan's heart palpitate.

When was the last time you sat down and cried before you prayed? Of course it's not always necessary that you weep before you pray, but when you face a situation serious enough to weep about, isn't that situation serious enough to pray about as well? Serious praying and serious weeping go hand in hand. Together they are an important part of the posture of empowered prayer.

Nehemiah Mourned

Here's a component to preparing our hearts and minds for prayer we don't often hear about these days—mourning.

What Nehemiah wrote in verse 4 is quite revealing. He said, "When I heard these things, I sat down and wept. For some days I mourned and fasted and prayed before the God of heaven." To Western minds there is little difference between weeping and mourning. But to the Eastern mind, the difference is real and significant. That's why these words frequently are distinguished from each other (2 Sam. 1:12; Mark 5:38; Rev. 18:11).

Weeping has to do with your eyes; mourning has to do with your whole body. Mourning (Hebrew, *abal*) is that loud wailing customary in the Middle East that you've probably seen on television. A tragic death in the Middle East is broadcast via satellite all over the world. In the funeral procession we see men carrying the casket, looking both somber and angry. They are followed by an entourage of women, wailing and screaming at the top of their lungs. Mourning in the Middle East is a physical and sometimes uncontrollable demonstration of grief.

In Western culture to mourn the way Nehemiah did may be out of character, even hypocritical. But mourning in your own way is still proper preparation for empowered prayer because mourning interrupts the normal course of life.

To give yourself to this kind of prayer you may have to take a morning or afternoon off from work. I have known people who got away from home for a few days just to weep and mourn and pray about something of gravity to them. That's posturing for prayer. That's one of the key elements in empowered prayer. That's making heart and mind preparation.

Nehemiah Fasted

Often fasting and prayer are linked in the Bible, but we are commanded to pray, not to fast. The only fast required by Moses was on the Day of Atonement (Lev. 23:27–32; Jer. 36:6). Still, godly people have always recognized the spiritual value of fasting. The Bible uses other terms for fasting such as afflicting the soul or denying yourself. Fasting to humble yourself before God was a part of life for pious Jews. Those who wanted to live godly lives accepted the intermittent denial of food as a way of getting close to God. Fasting was a good and godly practice. So it's not surprising that Nehemiah fasted to prepare himself mentally and spiritually for prayer.

But Jesus cautioned us not to fast as the Pharisees did. They did not use fasting to posture their hearts before God; they used it to be noticed by others. They made a parade of piety, which Jesus condemned (Matt. 6:16–18).

Although the Bible doesn't say we should always fast when we pray, I have found it an especially rewarding discipline when I face a big decision or a particularly difficult situation. You may find it helpful too.

Fasting is a private thing even if done in concert with others. Don't fast to impress anybody. Fasting is the fruit of piety, not a showcase for it. It's a meaningful way to prepare for prayer. But make sure your purpose is spiritual. If you fast to lose weight, don't call it a fast; call it a diet.

The next time you face a difficult situation or a bone crushing need, don't just jump into prayer. Assume a prayer posture. Get empowered to pray. Prepare your heart and mind before you prepare your prayer.

PIETY AND PRAYER

Piety and prayer. They're like peanut butter and jelly, Rogers and Hammerstein, fall weather and football. They go together. When we prepare to pray in a godly way, it's reasonable to anticipate we will pray in a godly way. Personal piety is reflected in the way we prepare ourselves for prayer, and that kind of preparation results in empowered prayer.

In the great prayers of the Bible, when there was time for thoughtful preparation there was also a thoughtful pattern to prayer. Not all prayers reflect this pattern, of course; not all prayers have the same intent. But if there is a general pattern to the prayers of empowered people, shouldn't there be a pattern to our prayers as well? Perhaps this pattern can best be remembered with the acronym A-C-T-S:

A doration
C onfession
T estimony
S upplication

Some understand the T to mean thanksgiving, but I prefer the broader meaning of testimony. Sometimes it takes the form of thanksgiving and sometimes it's telling what God has done for us. Either way, testimony is always rooted in thanksgiving.

I'll discuss this pattern later in this book, so I only introduce it in Nehemiah's prayer.

Adoration

Nehemiah began where prayer should always begin, with thoughtful reflection on who God is. His diary records, "O LORD, God of heaven, the great and awesome God, who keeps his covenant of love with those who love him and obey his commands, let your ear be attentive and your eyes open to hear the prayer your servant is praying before you day and night for your servants, the people of Israel" (Neh. 1:5–6).

Do these sound like the words of a pious man? Absolutely. The basis of piety, the foundation of godliness, is a recognition of who God is and who we are.

God is the God of heaven. He is the God who answers by fire. He is the regal Sovereign of the universe. While God is readily available to us (just a prayer away), he transcends us in power, wisdom, holiness, and in every way. He is not the false god of business or Wall Street. He is not the false god of phony religious charlatans. He is not the false god of the earth spirit. Our God is an awesome God, and his name is Jehovah.

If you want to be empowered when you pray, begin with adoration and praise, appreciation and worship. After all, prayer is not just about us; it's about God.

Confession

With his adoration expressed, Nehemiah's thoughts turned to his people and himself. What a contrast! A sovereign God and a sinful people. It's a contrast too striking to ignore.

Confession of sin follows worship in prayers of piety. Nehemiah continued to pray, "I confess the sins we Israelites, including myself and my father's house, have committed against you. We have acted very wickedly toward you. We have not obeyed the commands, decrees and laws you gave your servant Moses" (Neh. 1:6–7).

Piety—paying close attention to the things that please God—does not permit pliability in describing sin. Notice Nehemiah came right out with it. He called sin by its real name, not by the wimpy names we call it today. He didn't beat around the bush and neither should we when we confess our sins.

Confession is not only good for the soul, it is essential for empowered prayer. The Holy Spirit does not work through unclean vessels. He will not empower people with unconfessed sin. Don't make excuses. That's why posturing your heart and mind before you pray is so vital. It gets you in the right frame of mind to confess your sins.

Testimony

Most great prayers of the Bible contain some expression of testimony. As mentioned earlier, in many prayers this is also a time of thanksgiving. Testimony is a memory technique; it reminds us of what God has promised and what he has done for us.

"Remember the instruction you gave your servant Moses, saying, 'If you are unfaithful, I will scatter you among the nations, but if you return to me and obey my commands, then even if your exiled people are at the farthest horizon, I will gather them from there and bring them to the place I have chosen as a dwelling for my Name'" (Neh. 1:8–9).

Nehemiah combined a reminder of God's promises with a recitation of divine performance on Israel's behalf. I like that. That's not a bad idea for us. If you want power in your prayers, spend time rehearsing what God has promised you. Then follow that up with what he has already performed in your behalf. That's powerful stuff.

It's even a good idea to quote a little Scripture in your prayers. Tell God you remember what he said. Remind him of his promises, not that he needs reminding, but he delights in your being aware of them. And never neglect to thank him for how significantly he has already blessed you. Your prayers can be a powerful forum to rehearse God's faithfulness.

Supplication

Don't be put off by this big word. It just means to ask for something humbly and earnestly. I like the word. It's prayer with a capital P. It's also the last element in the A-C-T-S formula for empowered prayer.

This final feature of prayer is often the sum total of our prayers—humbly asking him for whatever is on your heart. Nehemiah prayed, "O Lord, let your ear be attentive to the prayer of this your servant and to the prayer of your servants who delight in revering your name. Give your servant success today by granting him favor in the presence of this man" (Neh. 1:11).

That's straightforward. He asked God to hear his prayer and give him success, to grant him favor in the presence of Artaxerxes, the Persian king. Nehemiah had a heart for Jerusalem. He was a true patriot, but he had no power in himself. He prayed God would open the door a tiny crack to the only man who could enable him to return to Jerusalem and rebuild the walls. Nehemiah asked God to remove the obstacles, to pave the way, to prepare the king's heart.

If you read the next chapter of Nehemiah's diary, you'll see God did all that and more. God does exceeding abundantly above all that we ask or think (Eph. 3:20).

Do you want to be empowered to pray? Don't rush into prayer. Prepare yourself as Nehemiah did. Stop what you're doing. Concentrate on God and your need. Spend the time necessary to insure that your audience before him is a meaningful one. You can afford to sing badly, spell badly, or speak badly, but you can't afford to pray badly.

You do not have to be a pastor, T.V. preacher, or theologian to pray well. But you do have to pray with genuine heart preparation. Invite the Holy Spirit to examine your motives and give you a contrite heart and a broken spirit. These are the keys to being personally prepared to pray—not flowery words or theological jargon. Ask God's Spirit to prepare you and you will be empowered to pray with skill.

ON-LINE PRAYER

When Nehemiah received the word of Jerusalem's crumbled condition, it was not a good day. But he was a man of piety and a man of prayer. He would not let disastrous news shake his character or keep him from talking with God. It wasn't a good day, but even when we don't have a good day, we can have a godly day.

What does it mean to be empowered to pray? It means taking the right steps to prepare yourself for a serious conversation with God. Preparation for prayer is more than gathering information. It's also preparing our hearts. We must be spiritually prepared as well as intellectually prepared.

How seriously we take prayer may well be reflected in how seriously we prepare to pray. Fortunately we don't have to prepare alone. We have a divine Helper (Rom. 8:26). The attention to details, the piety of personal preparation, the desire to pray in a biblical manner—these are the things the Holy Spirit uses to empower us to pray. Preparing yourself for prayer is as important as prayer itself.

Heavenly Father, the one worthy of our praise and piety, we pray to you as the God of perfection. You alone are worthy of our prayers. We are not sinless, Father, but we are serious. We want to please you. We want no impediments to prevent our prayers from reaching your heart. Prepare us, Father, through your Holy Spirit. Bring us personally to where we must be if we are to be heard by you. Make us godly people, and when we are not, make us ashamed. We genuinely love you, Father, as we love your Spirit and your Son, in whose name we pray. Amen.

When It's Time to Say You're Sorry

3

Daniel's Prayer
Daniel 9:1–19

Being empowered to pray means being cleansed of personal sin and thoroughly prepared to approach a holy God.

Preparing to pray is gathering data and posturing your own heart, but it's more. Sometimes there are obstacles that have to be cleared away before you pray. Failure to clear these obstacles means failure to pray with power.

One of the most stubborn obstacles is sin. When there are things in our lives that need to be confessed and forgiven, it's useless to pray until they're dealt with. If we cherish sin in our hearts, the Lord will not listen to our prayers (Ps. 66:18). So confession of known sin should be high on our prayer priority list. We need to spell it out to God and say we're sorry.

Do you remember the line from the film *Love Story*? "Love is never having to say you're sorry." That's nice sentiment, but it's not reality. Frequently love means saying you're sorry. Our relationships sour if we're unwilling to ask for forgiveness.

Ken and Marie know what that's like. Ken and Marie were young and in love. Marie was Ken's dream date. She was worth the effort to catch her because Ken thought Marie would make the ideal pastor's wife. Her father was a pastor. When Ken and Marie were married, they faced a lot of challenges but overcame them all. God blessed them with wonderful children. Ken became a pastor, and on the surface everything looked fine.

But that was just the surface. Ken constantly failed to live up to Marie's expectations. She laughed with him in public but berated him in private. They both were strong willed and rarely spoke kindly to each other. What was crumbling at home soon became evident to the church. Ken resigned as pastor, but it wasn't enough. There was no open door to forgiveness. There was no recognition of personal guilt. Ken and Marie divorced. Their ministry was over. They just never learned to say, "I'm sorry."

Daniel's prayer is one of the classic prayers of the Old Testament. It exemplifies both the proper preparation for prayer and the proper attitudes in prayer. In addition, it repeats the A-C-T-S formula, that pattern for prayer that pleases God.

Born to a noble family (Dan. 1:3, 6), Daniel was a young man—perhaps a teenager—when he was taken captive and carried into Babylonian captivity. He spent most of his life as a prisoner in a foreign land.

Have you ever been challenged to pray about something you noticed during your Bible reading? I think prayer precipitated by God's Word is the most exciting prayer of all. That's what happened to Daniel. One day reading his Bible (Dan. 9:2), he was startled by something he read in Jeremiah. Daniel discovered that the captivity of the Jews would only last seventy years (Jer. 25:11–12). He got out his pocket calculator and estimated the Israelites had been in captivity sixty-six years already, so their national ordeal was almost over. Only four more years. Hallelujah!

We all respond to startling discoveries in different ways. How do you think Daniel responded to his exciting discovery? Did he (a) call a news conference, (b) schedule a caterer and announce a lavish celebration, (c) write a book on prophecy, or (d) none of the above?

You got that one right, I know.

Daniel's discovery was too important to trivialize. He said, "So I turned to the Lord God and pleaded with him in prayer and petition, in fasting, and in sackcloth and ashes" (v. 3). Daniel went immediately to prayer.

I find what Daniel said in his prayer and the way he said it helpful in my own praying. Daniel's prayer is a paragon of prayer, a prototype for empowered prayer, the kind of prayer God likes to hear and answer. Let's learn the skill of prayer from someone who knew how.

Daniel's Preparations for Prayer

We've already seen that prayer is empowered by God through preparation. There are times when we can do little more than shoot up a prayer to God, but those occasions are rarer than we'd like to admit. Most of the time we have ample opportunity to prepare for serious prayer.

The components of Daniel's preparation are mentioned in verse 3. He turned his attention to the Lord, he fasted, he put on sackcloth and covered himself with ashes. Since we have already investigated some of these actions in Nehemiah's preparations, let's briefly note them and move on.

Daniel Concentrated on God

Of all the old hymns about prayer, the lyrics of William Runyan's "Lord, I Have Shut the Door" seem most appropriate here:

> Lord, I have shut the door, speak now the word
> Which in the din and throng could not be heard
> Hushed now my inner heart, whisper thy will
> While I have come apart, while all is still.

If you've had the dubious pleasure of courting in the presence of younger siblings, you can surely appreciate the meaning of this hymn. When my wife Linda and I were dating, her two younger sisters seemed to be everywhere. If we sat on the couch, they were right there on my knees. If we went for a walk, they were our shadow. If I tried to put my arm around her, they surfaced between us like a waterspout. We laugh about it now, but when I was nineteen I could have drop-kicked both of them.

Surely our most intimate times with someone we love are when we're alone. That's true with God too. Being alone with God, shutting everyone else out, helps us to concentrate in prayer.

Alexander Hamilton once said, "Men give me some credit for genius. All the genius I have lies in this: When I have a subject in hand, I study it profoundly. Day and night it is before me. My mind becomes pervaded with it. Then the efforts that I make are what people are pleased to call the fruits of genius. It is the fruit of labor and thought!"

Do you suppose those famous "prayer warriors" you've read about weren't geniuses at all? Is it possible they were just people who had learned how to concentrate when they prayed? If you want to be empowered to pray, do what Daniel did. When he turned to the Lord God, his heart and soul, his eyes and ears, his spirit and psyche all converged on God. It was as if no one else existed—only God and he.

Daniel Got Serious

Daniel employed every known auxiliary to prayer. He fasted, put on sackcloth, and sprinkled ashes on himself.

Should you do this too? Likely you don't even own any sackcloth. What can you do to prepare for prayer that will demonstrate your seriousness? How about canceling your usual activities and spending the day alone with God? That's radical, but your need may be equally radical.

Are you facing a decision about changing jobs? Has your boyfriend asked you to marry him? Do you have cancer, and there are two very different treatments available to you, and the doctors have left the choice up to you? You've been invited to go to your son's home for Christmas and you wonder if it's a good idea. Have you inherited some money, and you're grappling with what God wants you to do with it?

These are the kinds of decisions that require serious prayer. Fasting may help you discern God's will. Taking time out to spend the day alone with God could be beneficial. Remember James' advice: "If any of you lacks wisdom, he should ask God" (James 1:5).

In the early days of the Back to the Bible ministry, Theodore Epp would go away for a week at a time, checking into a hotel with no T.V., radio, or entertainment. He was there to get alone with God and pray. When he came back to the broadcast office, everyone knew he had met with God. That's the kind of meeting we all need when faced with important decisions.

When you need divine wisdom, take whatever steps are necessary to be empowered to pray. Change your normal routine; go to a different place to pray; write a letter to God pouring out your heart; do something that is the modern equivalent of sackcloth and ashes.

Remember, today's preparation determines tomorrow's achievement. That's as true in praying as it is in everything else.

DANIEL'S CONFESSION

The attitudes Daniel brought to his prayer are the mirror image of Nehemiah's attitudes. He acknowledged the contrast between God's righteousness and Israel's guilt. He expressed both shame for Israel's sin and wonder at the mercy of God. But more than anything else, Daniel gave genuine confession. Daniel was honestly sorry about the sins of his people. "I prayed to the LORD my God and confessed" (Dan. 9:4). This great prayer of the Bible is as much confession as it is petition.

If you have something to confess to God in prayer, here's an excellent example of how to do it. While confessing Israel's sins, Daniel used no less than seven Hebrew words for sin. Reading his prayer is like sitting in Theology 101 class. All the major words are there, and they are power words. Let's take a look.

Missing the Mark

When an archer pulls back on the bowstring and lets his arrow fly, his intent is to hit the bull's-eye. If he doesn't, he has missed the mark.

God's holiness requires perfect righteousness. He compares everything to his righteous standard. And what is God's perfect standard? It's not the law, not the church, not the rule of the majority. God's perfect standard is his Son, Jesus Christ, the Righteous One.

Jesus is God's bull's-eye. He is the express image of the invisible God (Col. 1:15). He is the glory of God, God in flesh (John 1:14). Little wonder when we compare our righteousness to his, we don't measure up. "For all have sinned and fall short of the glory of God" (Rom. 3:23).

Daniel affirmed this when he said, "We have sinned" (Dan. 9:5), missed God's mark (Hebrew, *chatta*). Daniel was clearing away any obstacles to being empowered by God. He confessed the sin of God's people (vv. 5, 8, 11, 15, 16, 20) because he wanted nothing more than he wanted God's power in prayer.

Iniquity

When Daniel said, "We have . . . done wrong," he was admitting Israel's iniquity. They had bent the rules of God. Daniel chose a word (Hebrew, *'awon*) that means to pervert or make crooked (vv. 5, 13, 16). Israel chose to walk in their own way. They made up their own rules. They bent God's rules to suit their own purposes.

Sound familiar? Look around you. We've done that; our society does it all the time. If we want to be empowered to pray, we have to be clean before God. Power and purity go hand in hand.

Become transparent with God. Tell him the wrong you've done. Be specific. Naming the things you've done and confessing them is God's design for forgiveness. "If we confess our sins, he is faithful and just and will forgive us our sins and purify us from all unrighteousness" (1 John 1:9).

Don't let unconfessed iniquity rob you of power in prayer.

Wickedness

Daniel's third expression of sinfulness was "we have been wicked" (vv. 5, 15). This word (Hebrew, *resha'*) reflects an attitude rather than an action.

Frequently the Bible describes our restlessness without God. We have a big God-shaped void in our lives. That's what Daniel was confessing. Maybe it's what you need to confess to be empowered to pray.

Isaiah described the wicked as "the tossing sea, which cannot rest, whose waves cast up mire and mud" (Isa. 57:20). That's a pretty graphic image. Until we are at peace with God, we are like the tossing sea, unable to be calmed, able only to stir up mire and mud.

Augustine was like that. Born in A.D. 354, he had an appetite for wickedness. At age eighteen he took a live-in girlfriend who stayed with him for thirteen years. Augustine left Africa and went to Rome and then to Milan, drifting aimlessly. He dabbled in every kind of screwball philosophy and religion. Finally at age thirty-three, Augustine trusted Jesus Christ as Savior and found real peace and purpose in life. He confessed to God, "My heart was restless, until it found rest in you."

When you confess your restlessness to God, recite some of his great promises about peace (John 14:27; Rom. 5:1;

Phil. 4:7). Claim them. Cling to them. God will keep you in perfect peace if your mind is steadfast on him (Isa. 26:3).

Rebellion

Like a cup of coffee, Daniel's confession was filled to the brim. "We have sinned and done wrong. We have been wicked and have rebelled" (Dan. 9:5). That Israel had rebelled against Jehovah was not news. That was the sad story of Israel's long walk with God. The word Daniel chose in confessing "we have rebelled" (vv. 5, 9) means to disregard authority (Hebrew, *marad*).

Daniel knew rebellion against authority was natural. We know that too, don't we? Every time we choose our own path, go our own way, or disregard God's Word and follow the advice of friends or neighbors, we rebel against God. Daniel knew this rebellion had to be confessed as sin, and so do we. The question is not should it be confessed, but will it be confessed? Will you be empowered to pray or held powerless by rebellion?

Unfaithfulness

Daniel continued the litany of Israel's shortcomings. "You have scattered us because of our unfaithfulness to you" (v. 7). Unfaithfulness (Hebrew, *ma'al*) means falsehood or vanity.

Remember your childhood days? You know what the Hebrew word means. It's a cover-up. You spilled gravy on the new tablecloth and moved your plate over the stain to hide it. That's *ma'al*. We do the same thing as grown-ups but with a little more sophistication. A man comes home late from work. He's been doing that a lot lately. He attempts to cover up the affair he's having by telling his spouse that he's working late. Unfaithfulness. A betrayal of trust.

Daniel confessed that Israel had been two-faced. They had said they would obey God; they even went through the motions. But it was a cover-up, and no cover-up is ever successful with God. He sees right through them all.

Transgression

By now you can see how seriously Daniel took clearing away the clutter that would prohibit God from empowering him to pray. The sixth word he used in confession was transgression. "All Israel has transgressed your law and turned away, refusing to obey you" (v. 11). This transgression (Hebrew, *avar*) occurred every time Israel disregarded God's law and crossed over its boundaries.

Israel's lawlessness was generally deliberate. God said, "This far you may go and no farther." When Israel said to God, "Oh yeah! We'll do as we please," that was a deliberate transgression of the law. It still is.

Today many people have attitudes toward God that are seriously calloused. They seem to be saying to God, "Oh yeah! We'll do as we please." Abortionists hold up their choice placards and say to God, "Oh yeah! We'll do as we please." The homosexual community marches for gay pride and says to God, "Oh yeah! We'll do as we please." It's this callousness toward God that Daniel confessed as sin. We must do the same.

Evil

Finally, Daniel confessed his nation's guilt in all the calamities that had befallen them. The captivity was their own fault. They had not regarded God's commands; they chose evil (Hebrew, *rà*) and were paying the penalty for their choice.

Daniel admitted, "The LORD did not hesitate to bring the disaster upon us" (v. 14). But his spiritual insight shined through when he said, "for the LORD our God is righteous in everything he does; yet we have not obeyed him" (v. 14). The prophet did not attempt to blame God.

One of the surest marks of maturity is the ability to admit guilt. To say, "I'm sorry; I was wrong" ties more tongues than mothers tie shoes. It takes a mature Christian to confess sin in prayer.

When was the last time you agonized over your sin? Did you have trouble getting the words out in prayer? Don't worry. The ease with which we confess sin may be a clue to the genuineness of our confession. If you find it too easy, it may also be too shallow.

I'm the first to admit that this isn't very exciting stuff. Confessing sin never is. That Daniel used seven different Hebrew words to confess his sin may not be important to you. But confession is very important, for it's just this simple: no confession, no empowerment. Daniel understood how true this is. That's what makes his one of the great prayers of the Bible.

Is it time you said, "I'm sorry" to God? Ideally love is never having to say you're sorry. But we don't live in an ideal world. In this world, love is meaning it when you say, "I'm sorry." We have a long way to go, but prayer is the place to start.

DANIEL'S PATTERN FOR PRAYER

As we saw in Nehemiah's prayer—and will see again and again—there is a recurring pattern in the great prayers of the Bible. It's a pattern that places the emphasis on worship and adoration rather than on petition. Daniel's prayer is important to us not only because it reflects the need for confession but because it demonstrates the pattern for empowered prayer. Like Nehemiah, Daniel's prayer reflects the A-C-T-S pattern.

Adoration

This great prayer began where all great prayers begin—with God. Daniel knew he must confess his nation's sins, but before he got to that, he began with adoration to Jehovah.

"O Lord, the great and awesome God, who keeps his covenant of love with all who love him and obey his commands" (v. 4). What a beginning. When prayers begin this way, there's no telling how great they'll end.

Daniel expressed his appreciation for God's grandeur. Jehovah is the great God, the awesome God. He is the faithful God, one who keeps his promises and lives up to his covenants. The prophet also expressed his appreciation for God's character. "Lord, you are righteous. . . . The Lord our God is merciful and forgiving" (vv. 7, 9).

In his prayer Daniel contrasted God's righteousness with Israel's unrighteousness. Because God is just, he must deal justly with those who disregard his law, and Israel had done just that. On the other hand, God's mercy was contrasted with Israel's unfaithfulness. God is holy, but he is also tender and merciful. Daniel adored his God, and he wasn't embarrassed to tell God how he felt.

Confession

Empowered prayer begins by focusing on the stellar character of God but then refocuses on the sinful character of man. When we focus on God's character, we use a telescope, attempting to fathom anything we can about the sovereign God. But when we focus on our character, we use a microscope, spying out every microbe of sin that will spiritually debilitate us and rob us of power in prayer.

Daniel knew Israel's years in captivity were about to end. He had read his Bible, and he trusted it. But he also knew confession was a prerequisite to restoration.

In verse 6 Daniel acknowledged that God had sent prophet after prophet with message after message to head off Jerusalem's date with destruction. "We have not listened to your servants the prophets, who spoke in your name to our kings, our princes and our fathers, and to all the people of the land" (v. 6).

Any nation that shows little respect for God and those chosen to preach God's Word is poised precariously for the judgment of God. It was certainly true of Judah; it is equally true of America.

Have you ever pleaded with God for your country? Have you prayed for an alternative to judgment? How often have you confessed national sin in your prayers? Most Christians have not.

Among all the activist ways to reform your country, do not fail to learn about the effectiveness of empowered prayer. Some may consider praying for national revival an anemic exercise, but that's what has worked in the past, and it will work again.

Testimony

Daniel remembered Jehovah's faithfulness in bringing his forefathers out of Egypt (v. 15). He testified to God's history of redemption.

We could do the same in America. The testimony of God's blessings on America should be a part of every American Christian's prayers.

As an American, it's impossible to underestimate the ways in which answers have come to the prayer, "God, shed his grace on thee." But, ironically, those who have the most to be thankful for seem to be the least vocal in their thanks.

On April 30, 1863, President Abraham Lincoln made a proclamation for a national day of fasting, humiliation, and prayer in America. He said, "We have been the recipients of the choicest bounties of heaven. We have been preserved . . . in peace and prosperity. We have grown in numbers, wealth and power, as no other nation has ever grown. But we have forgotten God. We have forgotten the gracious hand which preserved us in peace and multiplied and enriched and strengthened us; and we have vainly imagined, in the deceitfulness of our hearts, that all these blessings were produced by some superior wisdom and virtue of our own."

Lincoln was right, of course, but he would have to be alive today to know just how right. Since testimony is part of the biblical formula for prayer, and since most of us have experienced so very much of God's goodness, isn't it time our prayers included greater recognition of what God has already done rather than a rehearsal of what we want him to do?

Supplication

Daniel concluded his great prayer with serious supplication. If you love your nation, you cannot read verses 16–19 without a lump in your throat:

O Lord, in keeping with all your righteous acts, turn away your anger and your wrath from Jerusalem (v. 16).

Now, our God, hear the prayers and petitions of your servant. For your sake, O Lord, look with favor on your desolate sanctuary. Give ear, O God, and hear; open your eyes and see the desolation of the city that bears your Name (vv. 17–18).

O Lord, listen! O Lord, forgive! O Lord, hear and act! For your sake, O my God, do not delay, because your city and your people bear your Name (v. 19).

Notice the urgency in Daniel's prayer. It's as if his enemies were at the door ready to carry him away. He heard the approaching footsteps. Nevertheless Daniel took the time to prepare himself to pray. He made a detailed confession of sin. He supplicated for God's mercy and forgiveness. Little wonder his prayer was empowered by God.

When it's time to say "I'm sorry; please forgive me," there is no more appropriate place to begin than at the footstool of God. Both individually and nationally we have treated God poorly. We have sinned against the holy God. We need to confess our sin and seek his forgiveness. Prayer is the best way to do that.

ON-LINE PRAYER

What does it mean to be empowered to pray? It means to be cleansed of personal sin and thoroughly prepared to approach a holy God. "Who may ascend the hill of the LORD? Who may stand in his holy place? He who has clean hands and a pure heart" (Ps. 24:3–4).

One of the major components of the great prayers of the Bible is confession. We confess our own sins in personal preparation, and we may continue in confession by adding the sins of our family, church, and nation.

Father in heaven, Holy One of Israel, you alone are capable of forgiving our sin, and we thank you for hearing our prayer. We freely admit our shortcomings. We have sinned. We have cheated you of our love, we have skimped on our devotion to you, we have forsaken you as a nation. We have harbored bitterness toward others. We have spoken unkind words to our family. We have questioned your authority in our lives. We confess these things as sin. Please accept our sorrow with our confession. We ask in the authoritative name of Jesus our Savior. Amen.

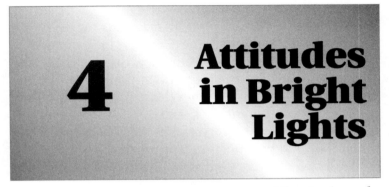

4 Attitudes in Bright Lights

*Pharisee's and
Tax Collector's Prayers
Luke 18:10–14*

*Being empowered to pray means approaching God
with an attitude of true humility.*

It's the latest national elixir, said to cure everything from bad grades to drug addiction. I'm talking about self-esteem. We're being immersed in a "love me" mentality. Recent best-selling books have told us we need to affirm ourselves and help others recognize the good in themselves. Businesses and schools are giving away more awards and holding more recognition services than ever before in an attempt to make people feel good about themselves—even if they are unproductive on the job or failing in the classroom.

A University of Michigan psychologist noticed that American schoolchildren ranked their abilities in math far ahead of students from Japan, Taiwan, and China. Unfortunately, their self-esteem was the only thing inflated; their math performances were woefully below those of the other countries.

This feel-good-about-yourself craze has cut deep into the fabric of the church. Some preachers have discovered that speaking of low self-esteem is less distasteful to their congregations than speaking of sin. One large interdenominational church preaches that sin is just the failure to live up to our potential. They consider chastising sinners as counterproductive: It makes them feel worse about themselves and produces underachievers.

To all this the holy God says, "Baloney!"

Of course, man is the crown of God's creation. We are created in his image, made after his spiritual likeness. That is not to be discounted. And for the Christian, we have something going for us that's even better. We are saints, the children of God, heirs of God, and joint-heirs with Christ. That's an inheritance that gives rise to a sanctified and proper sense of self-esteem.

But we must avoid false sources of self-esteem. Many today have been told there is a divine spark within them, and their self-esteem has soared as a result. But that's a humanistic esteem, a religion in which man is the center of his own universe. That's an esteem that anesthetizes the conscience and blinds the eyes to the consequences of personal sin. It's the kind of esteem that leads to hell.

A parable in Luke 18 provides the most striking example of someone blinded by feeling good about himself. Here the Lord contrasted a self-esteeming Pharisee with a tax collector suffering low self-esteem. They could just as easily have been a computer programmer and a businessman. Both men prayed, and God took note of their prayers.

Have you noticed that even when you try to conceal your attitudes, something always reveals them? The prayers of these two men displayed their attitudes in bright lights. The prayer of one man was filled with self-esteem; the prayer of the other was filled with sincerity. One man was empowered to pray by God; the other was only powerful in his own eyes.

There's something to be learned from each prayer about the relationship between empowerment and attitudes.

THEIR ATTITUDES ABOUT THEMSELVES

> To some who were confident of their own righteousness and looked down on everybody else, Jesus told this parable: "Two men went up to the temple to pray, one a Pharisee and the other a tax collector. The Pharisee stood up and prayed about himself: 'God, I thank you that I am not like other men—robbers, evildoers, adulterers—or even like this tax collector. I fast twice a week and give a tenth of all I get.' But the tax collector stood at a distance. He would not even look up to heaven, but beat his breast and said, 'God, have mercy on me, a sinner.'"
>
> Luke 18:9–13

Today we use the word *Pharisee* in a derogatory manner. To be a Pharisee is to feign virtue you do not have; it's to be a hypocrite, a fake. But this was not always the case. The Pharisees were much like a fraternal order or religious society. They took the interpretations of the law—made by their buddies, the scribes—and devised practical applications for those interpretations.

Their meticulous attention to the most minute details of the law, combined with their blindness to the big picture of life, earned the Pharisees the reputation of being self-righteous. They saw the foibles of others, but they were blind to their own large failings.

Clashes between Jesus and the Pharisees were frequent and often bitter. He called them a brood of vipers (Matt. 3:7) and said they were spiritually related to their father, the devil (John 8:44). In turn, they accused him of blasphemy (Luke 5:21) and attempted to trap him into contradicting the law (Mark 12:14).

Regardless of what Jesus thought of them, the Pharisees felt pretty good about themselves. Today we would say they enjoyed high self-esteem. They viewed themselves as keeping every ordinance of the law.

On the other hand, there was the tax collector. His self-esteem was lower than the dust under a snake's belly. He skulked, stood in a corner where he was less likely to be seen, kept his head bowed in shame. He was a prime candidate for a psychiatrist. He was also very much loved by God.

So two men came to the temple to pray. One was very self-assured of his religion, his status in the community, and his station before God. The other was not assured of anything. He was mistrusted by the Romans and hated by his own people. There could hardly have been a sharper contrast than between this Pharisee and tax collector. These everyday people provide the perfect example of right and wrong attitudes in prayer. One was empowered by God; the other was empowered by self-esteem. One succeeded in prayer; the other failed.

THEIR ATTITUDES TOWARD OTHERS

The temple was more than a place for public religious services. It was the place for Jerusalem's Jews to hang out.

It was the center of cultural and social life as well as religious life. No one was surprised to see the Pharisee there.

What was strange, and what must have surprised the Pharisee, was that the tax collector was there. He came for exactly the same reason—to pray.

The prayers of the two men betrayed attitudes toward others. The Pharisee prayed, "God, I thank you that I am not like other men" (v. 11). What a revealing admission. His self-esteem was intact; it was his esteem for others that suffered.

Can't you hear the pride in his words, "God, I thank you that I am not like other men"? The Pharisee thought he was not like other men, weaker men, spiritually impure men like robbers, evildoers, and adulterers.

The Pharisee was actually all the things he despised. He was a robber, robbing God of the glory due his name. He was an evildoer, a dishonest person, misrepresenting himself to those around him. He was likely not an adulterer—not literally anyway—but his departure from the Lord was the greatest adultery of all (Hosea 1:2; 5:3). The Pharisee was all that he hated, but blinded by his own self-esteem he could not see his sin.

He had no difficulty, however, seeing sin in others. He spotted the tax collector across the courtyard. The Pharisee added to his list of the religiously despicable "or even like this tax collector" (v. 11). Have you met people like this Pharisee in church? They have trouble seeing any point of view but their own. They spotlight their attitudes when they pray. They look down their spiritually elongated noses at newer Christians who haven't yet achieved victory over an old habit. In fact, they are forced to look down on everyone, for they see no one to look up to.

Victor was like that. He was the Sunday school superintendent in a church numbering about 125, and he had no trouble getting his way. Victor quickly befriended new couples attending church. He greeted everyone with a broad smile and a hearty handshake. But it wasn't long until Victor, who had the "gift" of criticism, began to examine every action and scrutinize every word of these newcomers.

In time the church grew tired of Victor's attitude. When the pastor resigned, Victor rose before the congregation and announced that the church didn't need to call another pastor. He was capable of being the spiritual leader of the church. Victor almost succeeded in his ecclesiastical coup d'etat, but several people mustered enough courage to ask him to leave the church.

Attitudes in bright lights.

The tax collector also betrayed an attitude toward others. When he entered the temple complex, he immediately searched out a far-off corner in which to pray. He didn't want to call attention to himself. He was there to do business with God. His attitude toward those around him was evident—and just the opposite of the Pharisee's.

The Pharisee likely walked right to the entrance of the Holy Place when he came to the temple to pray. He wanted to be seen by men, and there was no more public showcase than that. The tax collector stood at a distance across the courtyard. He didn't want to be seen by men. Each man got what he wanted: The Pharisee was seen by the crowd. The tax collector was heard by God.

THEIR ATTITUDES TOWARD GOD

Comparing himself to those around him, the self-righteous Pharisee looked pretty good. But how would he compare himself to Jehovah? How would he measure up when he stood next to El-Elyon, the Most High God?

As you might expect of a person with such high self-esteem, he even thought he looked pretty good when compared to Jehovah. "I fast twice a week and give a tenth of all I get" (v. 12).

In the first half of his pompous prayer the Pharisee compared himself with others. He came off smelling like a rose, or so he thought. In the second half he compared himself with God's law—in effect, with God's righteousness. He felt he was worthy to stand in the presence of a righteous God.

The Pharisee reminded God of all his righteous deeds. What the Pharisee did was more than the law required. As mentioned earlier, the law of Moses required fasting only on the Day of Atonement. Before the Babylonian captivity, this was the only regular day of denial (Lev. 16:29–31; 23:27–32). Fasting twice a week, every week, was the Pharisee's way of showing God he was super-religious. He took God's requirement and added to it a demonstration of his piety.

In addition, the Pharisee gave a tenth of all he had. This was another case of supererogation, going above and beyond the call of duty. Deuteronomy 14:22–23 outlines the principle of God's tithe for Old Testament Israel. God required a tenth of the grain of the field. Jesus said the super-spiritual Pharisees also tithed their mint, rue, and other garden herbs (Luke 11:42). In other words, to insure that he did not break any part of God's law, the Pharisee even tithed of his little garden at the side of the house. What dedication to detail!

But what hypocrisy! He was so proud of himself this Pharisee couldn't help reminding God he did all God required and more. He was no underachiever. He held his head high as he prayed in the most conspicuous place in the temple courtyard.

What a contrast was the lowly publican. He, too, entered the temple to pray. He, too, displayed an attitude toward God, but it was a humble attitude. "He would not even look up to heaven, but beat his breast and said, 'God, have mercy on me, a sinner'" (v. 13).

This tax collector was so humble he even refused to look toward God. He didn't want to be seen by the crowd, so why would he want to be seen by God? He beat himself on the chest in a demonstration of his shattered self-esteem. He wasn't worthy to stand before God, and he knew it.

The attitudes we bring to God can make the difference between being empowered to pray or not. Do you come to prayer as the publican, filled with esteem for God and desiring his power? Or do you come as the Pharisee, filled with esteem for yourself and desiring to demonstrate your power? God delights in answering the prayers of those who esteem him.

THE RESULTS

Prayer is not a matter of the lips only. It's primarily a matter of the heart. The words of our lips can fool others, but they cannot fool God.

Sometimes we're like that Pharisee. What came out of his mouth was what was in his heart. He spoke truly. He believed he was better than those around him. He was so wrapped up in himself that when it was time to pray, what was on the inside spilled out.

That's what makes the contrast with the tax collector so striking. The tax collector was emptied of himself. He only mentioned himself once in his brief prayer, and that in the objective case, "me." The Pharisee mentioned himself four times, all in the subjective case, "I." This tax collector knew he couldn't impress the Father, so he confessed to him instead. His humility was the cornerstone of his prayer. No prayer shawl is more appropriate than the shawl of humility.

Two men went up to the temple to pray. One prayed to himself about himself. The other prayed to God about himself. One man expounded on his greatness. The other exhibited his humility. Jesus said that one went home justified before God, the other didn't.

The tax collector humbly asked God to forgive his sins, and God graciously did so. God pronounced that he was righteous. His sins were blotted out (Ps. 51:1–2), removed as far as the east is from the west (Ps. 103:12), cast into the depths of the sea (Micah 7:19). What a feeling of esteem he must have had then!

You have a choice between humanistic self-esteem or imputed righteousness—take the righteousness. It will lead you all the way to heaven. The Pharisee's self-esteem leads elsewhere.

Two men. Two prayers. Two results.

Notice that each prayer was true. Each man described himself, and neither lied. The Pharisee described himself as righteous, and in his eyes he was. The tax collector described himself as a sinner, and he was.

Each prayer revealed to God the expectations of the man praying. The Pharisee was expecting honor, the tax collector, punishment.

The Pharisee came with Little Jack Horner's attitude: "What a good boy am I." The tax collector came with hymnwriter Augustus Toplady's attitude: "Nothing in my hand I bring. / Simply to thy cross I cling."

Both prayers were brief. In fact, they were so brief neither of them displayed the A-C-T-S formula. Each addressed God at the beginning and while the Pharisee's prayer was much longer, he never came back to God.

Neither prayer spent time in adoration. The tax collector's prayer gave no testimony to God's work in his life, but neither did the Pharisee's prayer. The tax collector's prayer was marked by confession; the Pharisee's prayer was not. The tax collector's prayer was marked by supplication; the Pharisee's prayer was not.

> Two went to pray? Oh, rather say
> One went to brag, the other to pray;
> One stands up close and treads on high
> Where the other dares not send his eye;
> One nearer to God's altar trod,
> The other to the altar's God.
>   Richard Crashaw

Before you set out to pray, check your heart. Are your attitudes smug, self-righteous, and like those of the Pharisee? Do you possess so much self-esteem that you fail to see that it's only by the power of Jesus' name you are permitted to speak to God?

Do you come to God with the attitudes and actions of the Pharisee, standing in a place of prominence but praying to yourself about yourself? Think about the last time you prayed. If you asked God which of these two men he thought you most resembled, what do you think he would say?

ON-LINE PRAYER

What does it mean to be empowered to pray? It means approaching God with an attitude of true humility. Jonathan Edwards said, "Nothing sets a person so much out of the devil's reach as humility." If you want Satan to be at your elbow when you pray, pray like the Pharisee. If you want him to keep his distance, pray like the tax collector. Prayer without humility is like bidding at an auction without money. It's all talk.

When we pray, it's not important who we are; it is important who God is. We must come to God in humility because regardless of our position in life—prince or pauper—we are nothing apart from Christ before the eternal God. If our attitude reflects that, we will be empowered to pray.

Dear God and Father—it's humbling even to address you in that tandem—God and Father. You are to be esteemed so much, we so little. And yet, you are our heavenly Father. We bear a unique relationship with you. Our attitudes toward others have not always been as humble as they should have been. Our attitudes toward you have secretly been worse, unworthy of your holiness. Help us, Father, to achieve what the tax collector had—a real sense of humility before you. We request this in the name and authority of your Son, Jesus, who alone gives meaning to our life. Amen.

Part 2

MAKING REQUESTS

5 Praying for Forgiveness

Jesus' Prayer
Luke 23:33–43

Being empowered to pray means feeling the relief of God's forgiveness and the joy of forgiving others.

To err is human; to forgive is not company policy! Imagine if this were true of God. There would be little reason to pray. But while the world is not a forgiving place, Scripture says, "You are kind and forgiving, O Lord, abounding in love to all who call to you" (Ps. 86:5).

"You are a forgiving God, gracious and compassionate, slow to anger and abounding in love" (Neh. 9:17).

If you have been injured, slandered, or hurt by someone, do you know how to ask God to forgive them? Praying forgiveness for others is not easy. It takes special grace and empowerment from God, but it is possible. Let's find out how.

The prayers of Jesus are all wonderful examples of the great prayers of the Bible. Each gives insight into how to pray with power. But the one that teaches us most about his heart is a prayer for forgiveness. Recorded in Luke 23:34, it's Jesus' prayer whispered to the Father while he endured the torture of the cross.

The Bible is incredibly concise in stating eternal truths. What takes scholars volumes to explain, the Bible often says in a few words.

The whole of creation, for example, was briefly explained in one statement—"In the beginning God created the heavens and the earth" (Gen. 1:1). The long-anticipated Messiah was introduced in one brief declaration—"Look, the Lamb of God, who takes away the sin of the world" (John 1:29). The answer to the quest for eternal life was summed up in just a few words—"You must be born again" (John 3:7).

When Luke recorded Jesus' agonizing death, he said, "When they came to the place called The Skull, there they crucified him, along with the criminals—one on his right, the other on his left" (Luke 23:33). The physician used his words sparingly. No elaboration. Just the facts.

I have a friend who is a great conversationalist. He never seems to be at a loss for words. When we talk, I always enjoy listening to him. Someday I even hope to have the opportunity to say something.

Genuine conversation, however, is never one-sided. It always involves give and take. He said; she said. When Jesus suffered on Calvary's cross, he wasn't silent. He was as a lamb before the slaughter only in that he offered no defense. He conversed with those on the ground and those hanging beside him. He even prayed, talking with his

Father. The conversation went both ways with those around him. He received a variety of responses, including repentance from one of the thieves and ridicule from the other. When the repentant thief prayed, Jesus responded.

To fully appreciate Jesus' Calvary prayer we must see it in the context of those who responded to it, and how they responded. So let's go back to that historic day outside Jerusalem's walls.

JESUS' PRAYER OF FORGIVENESS

All that Jesus said at Calvary is referred to as the seven last words from the cross. Not all seven statements are recorded in any one Gospel, but by comparing the Gospels we can suggest the following order.

Between 9 A.M. and noon Jesus said:

1. "Father, forgive them, for they do not know what they are doing" (Luke 23:34).
2. "I tell you the truth, today you will be with me in paradise" (Luke 23:43).
3. "Dear woman, here is your son," and to the disciple, "Here is your mother" (John 19:26–27).

From noon until 3 P.M., the three hours of darkness, no words were recorded.

About 3 P.M. Jesus said:

4. "My God, my God, why have you forsaken me?" (Mark 15:34).
5. "I am thirsty" (John 19:28).
6. "It is finished" (John 19:30).
7. "Father, into your hands I commit my spirit" (Luke 23:46).

Jesus' words from the cross were equally divided between the needs of others and his own needs. Two of his statements were addressed to no one in particular (John 19:28, 30); two were addressed to individuals (Luke 23:43; John 19:26–27); but three were addressed to the Father (Luke 23:34; Mark 15:34; Luke 23:46). When at the very door of death, Jesus knew whom to talk to.

Let's focus on the first of our Lord's final words—the words of forgiveness. They teach us how to be empowered to pray. It is fitting that in his final prayer, the one who came to seek and save the lost said, "Father, forgive them, for they do not know what they are doing."

WHAT IS FORGIVENESS?

The willingness to forgive is growing in our society. It has to; there is so much to forgive. Television and radio preachers are caught red-faced in sin. They shed a few tears, ask forgiveness, and go on with their ministries as if nothing happened. Pastors break God's rules and keep silent about it. When caught, they confess it before the church, look for forgiveness, and continue their ministries.

Something has gone seriously wrong with forgiveness. The word has been gutted of its meaning. Forgiveness is not an emotional response to sin. When people wrong me, I don't forgive them because I feel bad for them. In fact, my feelings are irrelevant. Hanging there in agony, Jesus did not ask the Father to forgive the mob because he had an emotional warm spot in his heart for them. His prayer ran much deeper than that. Forgiving was not the emotional thing to do, but it was the right thing to do.

In addition, forgiveness is not merely looking the other way. It's not just shrugging off an offense. Your neighbor punches you in the nose. You know you shouldn't punch him back. That's not the proper response. But neither is saying, "I know you didn't mean it. Let's just forget about it." That may be expedient, but it's not forgiveness.

Forgiving is not the same as forgetting. People have probably told you, "Forgive and forget." That's good advice, but can you forget? Have you programmed your mind only to retain the pleasant things and forget the unpleasant things? Of course not. It's not always possible to forget. Sometimes it's next to impossible.

Only God can forget sin. Only his infinite mind has the ability to willfully forget. God promised, "I will forgive their wickedness and will remember their sins no more" (Jer. 31:34). But we can't make that promise. We may forgive and often do. We may continue to remember, however, because forgiving is much more than forgetting. Often the two don't occur together.

Jesus couldn't just shrug off what the mob did to him. He couldn't simply look the other way. And he certainly couldn't forget about it. He had to pray that God would forgive those who offended him. He had learned the secret of forgiveness, and so must we.

Forgiveness Is a Choice

Forgiveness is an act of the will. It's a choice. It's not an emotional response to a situation; it is a volitional response to a person. Jesus' prayer of forgiveness makes that clear.

Judas betrayed the Master with a kiss. The cronies of the chief priests and elders bound him and led him away from his place of prayer, the Garden of Gethsemane. The Sanhedrin conducted an illegitimate trial in which false witnesses were assembled to testify against Jesus.

Peter denied his Lord three times. Pilate didn't have enough backbone to release Jesus when he knew the Savior was innocent. The crowd wanted a notorious criminal to be released instead of the innocent Lamb of God.

The crown of thorns, the torturous trek to the place of The Skull, the nails in his hands and feet, the jeering crowd—all these indignities were heaped on Jesus, and what did he do? He prayed, "Father, forgive them, for they do not know what they are doing."

Was he responding in anger? Was he responding with emotion? Was he simply looking the other way, shrugging off these injustices? Not in the least. He was praying his heart. He was expressing his will, making a choice. He was asking the Father to forgive those who had treated him so miserably.

An old proverb says we are most like beasts when we kill. We are most like men when we judge. We are most like God when we forgive.

Jesus prayed that God the Father would completely blot out the transgressions of these people. Blot out the record of those who spat in his face. Blot out the account of those who drove the nails in his hands and feet. Blot out the penalty for those who hated him enough to prefer Barabbas to the Lord of Glory.

Jesus' prayer was genuine. It was brief. It was offered on behalf of others. One of the final prayers of Jesus' life was a prayer of intercession for his torturers. He chose to forgive.

Forgiveness Is Your Choice

Does this impact you? It should. If you are sensitive to the Spirit of God, you cannot help but be moved by Jesus' heart in this his most difficult hour.

If Jesus concentrated on prayer on the day of his death, shouldn't we concentrate on prayer during the days of our lives? If he willfully forgave those who so shamefully mistreated him, can't we willfully forgive those who have mistreated us?

How have you been hurt? Has one of your children disappointed you, even disgraced you? Are you not speaking to that son or daughter? What about at church? Have you been criticized? Has something happened that you deem unforgivable? Is what happened to you more heinous than what the crowd did to Jesus?

The failure to forgive is one of the most enslaving traps in human existence. When we opt not to forgive those who hurt us, we become a slave not to the person but to our refusal to forgive. A little story illustrates this truth perfectly.

A little boy visiting his grandparents' farm was given his first slingshot. He was fascinated by it. What power was possessed in just a piece of wood and a strong rubber band. Daily he practiced his aim in the woods, but he could never hit his target.

One day after practicing, he returned to Grandma's backyard and spotted her pet duck. Without thinking, the boy impulsively took aim at the duck and let a stone fly. Finally Johnny hit something he aimed at; the duck fell dead.

The boy panicked. Desperately he hid the duck in a woodpile behind the shed. Just as he thought his ordeal was over, he looked up and to his horror saw his sister watching. He was devastated. Patty had seen the whole thing. She said nothing but ran to the house.

After lunch Grandma said, "Patty, let's wash the dishes." Patty replied, "Oh, Johnny told me he wanted to help do the dishes today, Grandma. Don't you remember, Johnny?" She then whispered in her brother's ear, "Remember the duck." So Johnny washed the dishes without a word.

Later that afternoon Grandpa asked if the children wanted to go fishing. Grandma said, "I'm sorry, but I need Patty to help make supper." Patty smiled and again said, "That's all taken care of. Johnny wants to do it, don't you, Johnny?" Again she whispered, "Don't forget the duck." So Johnny stayed while Patty and her Grandpa went fishing.

After a while Johnny couldn't take it any longer. He had done both his and his sister's chores, and the guilt was killing him. He blurted out tearfully, "I'm sorry, Grandma, but I killed your pet duck. I didn't mean to; it just happened."

"I know, Johnny," Grandma said, giving him a hug. "I was standing at the kitchen window and saw the whole thing. I love you and forgive you. But I was wondering how long you were going to let Patty make a slave of you."

Forgiveness is a choice. It's your choice. But so is prayer. What incredible power comes when these choices are synchronized. When we get the will to forgive and the will to pray in sync, we can move mountains of hurt. The mob that tortured Jesus wouldn't help him forgive. It was Jesus who was wronged, and it was Jesus who was willing to forgive. If you have been wronged, you are the one who must be willing to forgive.

Jesus voiced a prayer of forgiveness instead of a curse of condemnation. If we're to move mountains of hurt, we must be willing to do the same. Is there someone in need of your forgiveness today? If so, are you ready to pray with the same power as the Lord Jesus did? It's your choice!

THE RESPONSE OF THE CROWD

It's ironic that the innocent Jesus prayed for the guilty mob. Did they appreciate his forgiveness?

Luke is careful to record four distinct groups in the crowd that day. Most were just ordinary people (Luke 23:35). The rulers (v. 35) were there to oversee the executions. The soldiers (v. 36) were there to carry them out. The criminals on either side of Jesus (vv. 39–41) were there receiving justice. The response of these groups to Jesus' prayer—indeed to the whole crucifixion—was predictable. In fact, when you pray the prayer of forgiveness, you can expect the same response.

The Curiosity of the People

It was festival time in Jerusalem. The city's population had swelled as thousands from Galilee, the coastal plain, the hill country, and the Jordan Valley poured into the city for Passover. With so many Jews visiting Jerusalem, there was naturally a party air. Every year at this time the Roman governor would release a prisoner as a gesture of goodwill. But it was not uncommon in this festive atmosphere to include a crucifixion or two.

Crucifixions were frequent under Roman rule. The Jewish historian Josephus recorded in *Wars* (Book V) that the Roman general Varus crucified 2,000 insurgents in 4 B.C. The crucifixion of 3,600 Jews in A.D. 66 precipitated a rebellion.

But when Jesus went to the cross, this was no ordinary crucifixion. The people could feel it. They gathered at the place of The Skull on the road leading out of Jerusalem. That's where most crucifixions took place.

Rumor had it that this Jesus of Nazareth might be the Messiah. They didn't know for sure. They were curious. They were there because of the rumors.

The Sarcasm of the Religious Rulers

The rulers of the Jews took Jesus' claims more seriously. Matthew 27:41 identifies them as chief priests, teachers of the law, and elders of the people. Jesus had been a thorn in their side. They were the establishment; he was not. They lived in fine houses; he did not. Their lives were characterized by formality; his life was characterized by love. Jesus was everything they should have been, and more.

Consequently these leaders plotted against Jesus, looking for ways to kill him. They paid Judas to betray him. They sent soldiers to bind Jesus and take him from the Garden of Gethsemane. They tried him unlawfully. When Pilate asked what to do with Jesus, these people started the chant, "Crucify! Crucify!"

Their hatred for Jesus was now undiminished. As Jesus hung on the cross, they derided him. "He saved others; let him save himself if he is the Christ of God, the Chosen One" (Luke 23:35). They gloated over their success.

Jesus' prayer must have irritated these rulers. Imagine. He prayed that God would forgive the sins of the crowd. In their minds, it was Jesus who needed forgiveness. They responded to his prayer with more sarcasm.

The Taunting Roman Soldiers

The Jews called for Jesus' death, but it fell to the Romans to carry it out. Crucifixion was the Roman form of death; the Jews stoned people. It was not surprising, then, to find the Roman soldiers at the foot of the cross. They were doing their job—executing the condemned. It was a job some of them enjoyed only too much.

The Roman soldiers also taunted Jesus. But their taunts differed from the sarcasm of the Jews. While the religious leaders jeered at Jesus because he regarded himself as the Chosen One of Israel, the soldiers jeered at him because of the claim he was King of the Jews (v. 37). If Jesus was the King of the Jews, the Roman soldiers had come face to face with the one person who could challenge Roman authority in Palestine. That's why they laughed at him. How could he be king of anything?

The soldiers were unimpressed with Jesus' prayer. But the Roman eagle had met the Lion of Judah, and the Lion had won. From an elevated cross, he drew all men to himself with the words, "Father, forgive them." The prayer of forgiveness is evidence of divine empowerment.

The Discordant Criminals

Even the two criminals crucified on either side of Jesus hurled insults at him. Hearing the barbs of the religious leaders, one of the malefactors responded to Jesus' prayer, "Aren't you the Christ? Save yourself and us!" (v. 39).

The rulers addressed Jesus' relationship to God, facetiously calling him the Christ, the Chosen of God. The Roman soldiers addressed Jesus' relationship to the state, facetiously calling him the King of the Jews. But the criminal addressed Jesus' relationship to himself, facetiously suggesting that if Jesus could save himself, he could save these criminals too.

Both robbers scoffed at first. Matthew 27:44 says both heaped insults on Jesus. So does Mark 15:32. But eventually the criminals responded discordantly. Luke says they did not agree in their assessment of Christ. One continued his verbal abuse. The other criminal changed his tune.

But what changed him? Perhaps it was the genuineness of Jesus' prayer. The malefactor watched how Jesus handled the pain. He watched how he withstood the insults. The Spirit of God was working in his heart. And when the criminal heard the Lord pray for the Father to forgive him, it was too much for him. Prayer had proven too powerful a force. He was broken by forgiving prayer.

The man's response to Jesus' prayer was amazing. He rebuked the other criminal. He told his partner anyone facing the sentence of death should fear God instead of blaspheming an innocent man. Then he admitted his own guilt. "We are punished justly, for we are getting what our deeds deserve" (v. 41). He now had a clear vision of his sin, and it changed his destiny.

Finally he confessed the innocence of Christ. He believed that Jesus was who he claimed to be. The thief said, "This man has done nothing wrong" (v. 41). His faith was still in infancy, but it was real.

How we respond to Jesus tells us much about our relationship with the Father. The crowd responded in curiosity. The chief priests responded in ridicule. The scribes responded in satire. The elders responded in sarcasm. The Roman soldiers responded in derision. One thief responded in mockery. The other responded in faith.

If you have been wronged and are having trouble praying for those who have wronged you, you need to be empowered to pray. You need the same power Jesus demonstrated at Calvary. The good news is you can have it. Here's how.

First, remember that forgiveness is a choice. You either choose to forgive or not. The choice is yours. Jesus chose to forgive the mob. He could have been angry; yet he forgave. He could have been bitter; yet he forgave. He could have come down from the cross, yet he forgave. Forgiveness is a choice—your choice!

Second, prayer is a choice. Choose to pray for others when they wrong you instead of venting your anger. The prayer of forgiveness is the most gracious of all prayers. Perhaps you live in the midst of escalating hatred and hurt. There's only one way to deflate these emotions. Pray for your enemies.

Third, expect others to respond as the mob responded to Jesus' prayer. Be prepared. People haven't changed. Do you have friends, neighbors, or coworkers for whom you consistently pray? When they learn you are praying for their salvation, they may react as these did to Jesus' prayer for forgiveness. Most will laugh, some will mock, but thank God, some will believe. Keep on praying. Some will believe.

It would be easy to stop here, but Jesus' prayer was not the only prayer in this story. It was the major one, but after the response of those assembled at Calvary, there was another prayer. It was the prayer of the repentant thief. Jesus prayed for God to forgive others. The thief prayed for God to forgive him.

THE PRAYER OF THE FORGIVEN

Though brief, the thief's prayer was important. It proved he took Jesus up on the offer to be forgiven. When

Jesus prayed for the Father to forgive those huddled around the cross, this criminal said, "That's what I need." After he rebuked his partner and admitted his guilt, the repentant thief turned toward Jesus and prayed, "Jesus, remember me when you come into your kingdom" (v. 42).

Although not a classic statement of trust in Christ as Savior and Lord, it was effective. It demonstrated that he believed Christ was a king even though Christ now hung on a cross. The thief knew he was not worthy, but he certainly wanted eternal life.

Can we learn from this man's prayer? If we want to.

Notice that he addressed Jesus directly, either by name or as some manuscripts have it by the title "Lord." He knew whom he was talking to. This was not a deluded teacher hanging next to him. This was Christ the Lord, the Savior of the world. The repentant thief only wanted to be remembered by Christ. He didn't ask for salvation. He didn't know what salvation was. But he had faith in Christ and faith in the future. He petitioned, "Remember me when you come into your kingdom."

The thief's prayer was answered in a way he never would have guessed. If he had a lifetime to contemplate Jesus' response, he wouldn't even have come close.

THE RESPONSE OF THE SAVIOR

As the repentant thief contemplated the distant future, Jesus provided immediate hope. Jesus answered, "I tell you the truth, today you will be with me in paradise" (v. 43). This response was one of truth, immediacy, and expectancy.

The man was a criminal. He was used to lying and being lied to. But the moment of truth had come. Both

Jesus and he would soon be dead. The thief had just one opportunity to hear eternal truth. Jesus seized that opportunity.

"Today you will be with me in paradise." Today. Right away. Right now. Jesus responded to the man's faith immediately. There would be no purgatory, no trial period, no time to see if his faith was real.

The thief hoped for a small remembrance at some future date in Christ's kingdom. What he got was paradise that very day. That's the power of empowered prayer.

"Now to him who is able to do immeasurably more than all we ask or imagine, according to his power that is at work within us, to him be glory in the church and in Christ Jesus throughout all generations, for ever and ever! Amen" (Eph. 3:20–21).

ON-LINE PRAYER

What does it mean to be empowered to pray? It means feeling the peace of God's forgiveness and the joy of forgiving others. When he heard Jesus pray, the repentant thief had a change of heart and a change of destiny. The genuineness of the Master's prayer, its sincerity and self-lessness, had a profound impact on this hardened criminal's heart.

Have you been hurt beyond words? Is there someone who would benefit from your prayer of forgiveness? Then ask the Holy Spirit to give you the courage to forgive that person. Pray an empowered prayer. Remember, forgiveness is a choice. It's up to you. Jesus chose to forgive; so can you.

Every time I read the story of Jesus on the cross I am struck by one amazing fact. When the crowd was at its worst, Jesus was at his best. The crowd howled, "Crucify him! Crucify him!" They taunted the Savior, jeered at him, and mocked him. Still, he prayed for the Father to forgive them. When empowered by the Spirit of God, you can do that too.

Our Father in heaven, you are the one who has forgiven us of our sins. You are the one who provided atonement for us by the blood of your Son. You set the standard of forgiveness for all time. Thank you for forgiving me of my sin, both at the cross and on a daily basis. The blood of Jesus Christ keeps on cleansing me from all sin. Now Lord, there are others I must choose to forgive. It's my prerogative as a forgiven person. It's my choice. Help me to make the right choice. Thank you, in the power of your Son's name. Amen.

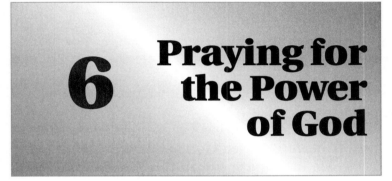

6 Praying for the Power of God

Elijah's Prayer
1 Kings 18:36–37

Being empowered to pray means praying to God with empowered petitions.

I don't know what to do. My situation is hopeless!"
Ever said that? Sure you have. What were you talking about? Your job? Your teenagers? Your finances? At times we all feel like our situation is hopeless. That's when we need to be empowered to pray.

Several years ago I was in Israel filming a video. Our crew had finished in Jerusalem, and we were to leave for Rome the next morning to film another video. Everything was in order. We had all the necessary permissions from the Italian government. All the fees were prepaid. The situation was flashing a green light.

But that night at my Jerusalem hotel, I received three faxes telling me the Italian government had suddenly and without explanation revoked our permits. My Italian contact said the only way we could get them back was to pay an additional $5,000 for him to broker them again for us. Something didn't smell right. It was time to pray for the power of God.

I called a friend who was a travel agent in Phoenix, Arizona. He initiated a three-way conference call with our contact in Rome. Imagine. An hour-long conference call between Rome, Jerusalem, and Phoenix—in the middle of the night!

While all this was being set up, I was on my knees. I have frequently needed God to demonstrate his power in my life, but never quite in this way. My prayer was simple. "Lord, work out every detail in a way that proves to everyone, even to governments, that you are God. And Lord, take the jitters away from me while you work." God enabled me to rest in quiet confidence. All the details weren't worked out over the phone, but when we arrived in Rome the next day all permits had been restored. The crew and I went about God's business as if nothing had happened. God answered my prayer.

The situation seemed hopeless, but hope was only a prayer away.

You and I aren't the first to be in what seems to be a hopeless situation. The prophet Elijah had a similar experience. His situation seemed hopeless, but he knew what to do. He needed to make a decisive call. He needed to take decisive action. He needed to pray a decisive prayer. And he needed a decisive response from God. He got all these in 1 Kings 18 where we see another of the great prayers of the Bible.

A Decisive Call

Ahab was king of Israel, but he was not much to write home about. He was guilty of more crimes against God than any of the kings before him. He married Jezebel, the daughter of the king of Sidon. Her name is synonymous with wickedness. She brought Baal worship to this unsanctioned marriage. To please his bride, Ahab built a temple for Baal in Samaria, and that greased the Jews' slide into apostasy.

Enter Elijah, the prophet of God.

Boldly he proclaimed God's judgment on Ahab's sin. Elijah declared that for the foreseeable future neither dew would rise nor rain would fall except at his command. Then Elijah disappeared.

For a nation whose economy was based on agriculture, this was not good news. The land had no rain for three and a half years. The situation was hopeless, or so everyone thought.

Finally Elijah went to Ahab to give him the chance to cry uncle. The prophet challenged the king to summon people from all Israel. They would gather on Mount Carmel for a contest between Ahab's 450 prophets of Baal and Elijah—450 wicked prophets against one flaming prophet of God. The odds were staggering.

When the people assembled, all eyes were on Elijah. The situation demanded a decisive call. In his loudest and most authoritative voice the prophet cried, "How long will you waver between two opinions? If the LORD is God, follow him; but if Baal is God, follow him" (1 Kings 18:21).

The word Elijah chose for *waver* means to hop or leap. Apparently the Jews had been hopping back and forth between Jehovah and Baal. Elijah knew it was time for them to make up their minds.

Sometimes we have trouble making up our minds. Should I have chocolate cherry cordial or butter brickle? But when it comes to Jehovah God and those who would challenge him, there's no room for indecision. "If the LORD is God, follow him; but if Baal is God, follow him." To fail to decide is to decide to fail. Indecision is not an option when it comes to God. We must choose.

A DECISIVE ACTION

What would Israel do? What would they say to this challenge? Nothing. They were paralyzed by their spineless wavering. Since the people didn't respond to Elijah's challenge, he had to take decisive action.

Elijah called for a test. Two bulls would be brought front and center. The 450 prophets of Baal would choose one; Elijah would settle for the other. Each would dress their bull and put it on the altar. No one would light the fire—that was the test. Jezebel's prophets would pray to Baal; Elijah would pray to Jehovah. "The god who answers by fire—he is God" (v. 24).

The test was eminently fair. In fact, the odds were in Baal's favor. Look at the numbers. Four hundred and fifty prophets to one, not to mention the four hundred prophets of Asherah who sat in Baal's cheering section. Look at the location—Mount Carmel. Carmel was thought to be the residence of Baal. It was his turf. He had the home court advantage.

Elijah even told the pagan prophets to go first (v. 25). They would have first crack at the fire. And if there was any advantage from the noontime sun, Baal's bunch had that as well (v. 26). Elijah stacked the deck on purpose. He wanted everyone to know that his situation was hopeless without Jehovah's intervention.

God sometimes does that. He allows the odds against your success to build so that when he makes you successful, the whole world knows he is God.

The contest got underway. The prophets of Baal chanted from early morning until noon. "O Baal, answer us! O Baal, answer us!" Again and again. But there was no answer.

Around noon Elijah saw this was going nowhere. He began to taunt Baal's prophets. "Shout louder! Surely he is a god! Perhaps he is deep in thought, or busy, or traveling. Maybe he is sleeping and must be awakened" (v. 27). Elijah couldn't resist needling them. He knew his God never slept. What was Baal doing? If he was a god, why didn't he answer?

The situation became as tense as a standoff between a bank robber and a SWAT team. These harried prophets began to slash themselves with swords and spears. Blood ran, and throughout the afternoon they continued their frantic prophesying, but to no avail. Verse 29 says, "But there was no response, no one answered, no one paid attention."

The prophets of Baal tried every trick in the book without response. Time was up. They had given it their best shot, and it wasn't good enough. It was now Elijah's turn.

Elijah rebuilt an alter that was dedicated to Jehovah but had been destroyed by the Israelites. Then he dug a trench around it. Elijah arranged the wood on the altar, laid the pieces of the bull on top, and then did something strange. He called for four large earthenware jars of water to be brought to the site and poured on the altar. Elijah said, "Do it again." And then a third time. With twelve huge jars of water, Elijah doused the altar until it was soaked and the water ran down, filling the trench.

The situation was hopeless. What would Elijah do? He needed the power of God, and he knew how to get it. He prayed!

A Decisive Prayer

Elijah's empowered prayer is recorded in 1 Kings 18:36–37. It's not a long prayer, but it teaches us what to pray for when our situation appears hopeless.

Elijah stepped forward, and in the hearing of all he prayed, "O LORD, God of Abraham, Isaac and Israel . . ." (v. 36). This accomplished two things:

First, it clearly signaled to the gathered crowd who Elijah's God was. His God was the real God. He was the God of Israel's patriarchs. The first of his Ten Commandments was "You shall have no other gods before me" (Exod. 20:3). There would be no mistake; Elijah was praying to the only God who could empower him.

But it accomplished something else. It told the Israelites that Elijah was not ashamed to pray to Jehovah in public, even among a hostile public. It didn't matter that everyone around him ridiculed Jehovah. He wasn't talking to them anyway. Elijah spoke boldly to his God.

We should never be ashamed to talk with God in a public gathering. When Jesus fed the five thousand, he took the five loaves and two fish and before he divided them or the multitude ate, "he gave thanks" (Matt. 14:19). Jesus prayed in public.

Paul was on his way to Rome when his ship encountered a horrendous storm on the Adriatic Sea. He tried to calm the fears of everyone on board by inviting them to have lunch. Acts 27:35 says, "He took some bread and gave thanks to God in front of them all. Then he broke it and began to eat." Paul prayed in public.

It's amusing to watch some Christians in a restaurant. They feel obligated to say grace over their meal, but they don't want to draw attention to themselves. So they give God a "headache prayer." They bow their head for a second or two and rub their forehead (so no one will see their eyes are closed). Not Elijah. He dramatically prayed in public. He was empowered to pray, and there was no question to whom he prayed.

But empowered prayer is not just loud or dramatic. It's not just public prayer. It's prayer that brings empowered petitions to God. It's prayer for the right things, things God is eager to grant. Let's notice what petitions Elijah included in his empowered prayer. All of them had to do with proof.

Proof That Jehovah Is God

"Let it be known today that you are God in Israel" (v. 36). Elijah's initial concern was not the success of his challenge but the integrity of his God. He wanted God to answer his prayer with fire to prove that he was indeed the God of Israel.

Is this the way you pray? Do your prayers reflect more concern for God or for your needs? Certainly God wants us to pray about our needs, but are your prayers self-centered? Think about what you've prayed for in the last week. How many times have your prayers concerned God? Do any of them prove your love for him, or do they just prove your need for his generosity? Elijah's deep concern was for God to prove to Israel that he, not Baal, was the real God. That's the kind of prayer God is eager to answer.

Proof That Elijah Was God's Spokesman

The prophet's second petition was hinged to the first. "Let it be known today that you are God in Israel and that I am your servant" (v. 36).

Elijah's fortunes were tied to Jehovah's. Elijah needed God's fiery response to prove that he was Jehovah's spokesman. If he spoke from Jehovah, he spoke the truth.

And if he spoke the truth, the judgment of God was about to fall on the prophets of Baal.

In many respects when we minister the gospel to others, our fortunes rise or fall with God's fortunes. If our hearers believe God, they will believe us. If they have little regard for God, they will have little regard for what we tell them about him. After all, we are ambassadors for Christ. Sure, we want to be believed when we witness for the Lord, but that's because we want our friends and family to come to Christ as Savior.

It's not selfish to pray that you will be believed. If you aren't believed, you aren't successful in winning others. Ask God to help those you seek to win to Christ to view you as an authentic ambassador for God. If they don't believe you, how will they believe him?

Proof That Elijah Acted in Jehovah's Behalf

There are good reasons for us to be somewhat tentative about trusting leadership today. This is true in every area of our lives—in church, in government, and in business. Many leaders have succumbed to greed. A few of our superstar religious leaders have been receiving exorbitant salaries from their ministries, living in the lap of luxury, and getting away with it until the day they came crashing down. They have made followers suspicious.

Perhaps Elijah was concerned about this. Being a spokesman for God always invited questions about sources, integrity, and motivation. Elijah prayed that the people would know "that I am your servant and have done all these things at your command" (v. 36).

When God calls you to do a work for him—whatever it is—you don't need your name on the marquee. For most of us that's not important. But you do need some proof that your motivation is pure, that you are acting in God's interest and not in self-interest. That's what Elijah was requesting. He wanted the people to know he was no showman, no charlatan, no self-aggrandizing stuntman. He was the servant of the living God, the God who answers by fire.

When you have pure motives in your service to the Lord, but that service is questioned, don't stew about it. Get empowered. Make the right petitions. Ask God to bless his work through your hands in a way that offers proof positive you have acted in his behalf. He may not answer by fire, but stand back anyway.

Proof That Jehovah Acted in Israel's Behalf

Elijah's final petition formed the conclusion to the supplication portion of his prayer. "Answer me, O LORD, answer me, so these people will know that you, O LORD, are God, and that you are turning their hearts back again" (v. 37).

These wayward Jews had to see it was Jehovah, not Baal, who acted in the best interests of Israel. Jehovah, not Baal, chose Israel to be his special people. Elijah's final empowered petition reflected his true love for his people. His heart was broken by their sin.

From our pulpits we hear that Jehovah is the healer of relationships, the answer to our financial woes, the lover of the downcast, the homeless, and the unborn. And all this is true. But these are only earthly skirmishes. The ultimate battlefield is the most basic question of all—who is God?

In our pluralistic society we may not want to offend those of other religions. As a result the twentieth-century pulpit has been strangely silent about the uniqueness of Jehovah God. He is not *a* god; he is *the* God, the only God. Jehovah is not just the Judeo-Christian God; he is the only God. There are not other names for God in other religious traditions—Allah, Buddha, the Great Spirit. Like Baal these are false gods in false religions.

Do you share Elijah's concern? Is it Jehovah who works in your behalf, or is it luck, science, Mother Nature, Karma, or any of the other false gods of our society? How loudly is your voice heard in challenging these false gods?

Perhaps it's time our voices issued a clarion call to follow God. Perhaps more of our prayers should ask God to demonstrate to wavering Christians that he is the God who answers by fire. Perhaps we need to pray about the most important issues, bring the most empowered petitions to God. Isn't it time your prayer life reflected the great battlefields of life and not just the mundane, daily skirmishes with need and want?

A Decisive Response

When we pray with power, God answers with "fire." When we pray with passion as Elijah did, when we offer empowered petitions about important issues, the fireworks will begin.

Verse 38 says, "Then the fire of the LORD fell and burned up the sacrifice, the wood, the stones and the soil, and also licked up the water in the trench." The response to Elijah's prayer was both decisive and immediate. There was no question that God had answered; everybody knew it. And the people responded to God.

The prophets of Baal had worked on their god all day. They prayed fervently, repeatedly. From morning until noon they shouted. From noon until the time of the evening sacrifice these false prophets slashed themselves, prophesied frantically, and prayed incessantly to Baal. But nothing happened.

Elijah prayed once to Jehovah, and Jehovah at once answered him. We don't always have our prayers answered immediately. Perhaps you have prayed for years without receiving an answer. The timing of God's answer is entirely up to him. But when Elijah prayed, God answered in a millisecond.

Not only was God's answer immediate, it was decisive. God sent fire from heaven so intense that the heat completely consumed the sacrifice. But God did more than Elijah asked. He's that kind of God. He does more than we can ask or imagine (Eph. 3:20). The fire also burned the wood on the altar that had been doused with water.

But hold on, there's more. The fire consumed the stones used to construct the altar as well. Even the dirt around the altar was scorched, and the water in the trench was licked up as if it were gasoline.

Jehovah had spoken. There could be no question who was God. The situation had seemed hopeless, but with God nothing is hopeless. Elijah knew that; that's why he prayed out loud, in public, when everyone else thought nothing could be done. God is in the business of doing what everyone believes can't be done.

How did the people react when they saw these heavenly fireworks? Verse 39 says, "When all the people saw this, they fell prostrate and cried, 'The LORD—he is God! The LORD—he is God!'"

Israel had changed their tune. This came as a result of a mighty display of the power of God, and that resulted from one man's prayer. Do you think one praying person can make a difference? Ask Elijah. When your situation appears to be hopeless, pray. And when you pray, give some extra thought to the motivations behind the petitions you bring to God.

ON-LINE PRAYER

What does it mean to be empowered to pray? It means praying to God with empowered petitions.

Elijah didn't pray that God would destroy his wayward people, but that he would convince them he was God. Why not ask God to demonstrate his power to your college student who is filled with questions? Ask him to prove to your unbelieving family that he is God. Ask him to bring your prodigal daughter home again. Ask him to heal wounded relationships in your church. The situation isn't impossible. It just needs your "flammable" petitions. When you take your empowered petitions to God, watch out! He's the God who answers by fire.

Dear Lord, God of all gods, God of heaven, who has no need to share his glory with the man-made gods of the earth, hear our prayer for a demonstration of your power. Show to an unbelieving world and a wavering church that you alone are God. Prove your spokesmen to be genuine, filled with your power and blessed by your hand. By your power show us the situation is not hopeless. Answer, O Lord, so our family and friends will know that you are God. In the name of the Savior. Amen.

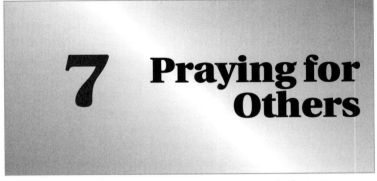

7 Praying for Others

Elisha's Prayer
2 Kings 6:8–23

Being empowered to pray means showcasing the needs of others in your petitions.

I'm married to a grandmother. When my children began having children, strange things began to happen. Telephone calls across the country occurred with great frequency. Toy stores had to add salespeople. Pictures of my grandchildren began falling out of Bibles, purses, and off the refrigerator door.

You can always recognize a grandmother. She's the baby-sitter who watches the kids instead of the television. I'm thankful for my grandchildren; in addition to all the happiness they add to my life, they give me little people to pray for.

But they're not the only people I pray for. My prayer list has three major categories: family, ministry, and others. Praying for others is one of the great privileges of the Christian. Twice Paul said to the Thessalonians, "Brothers, pray for us" (1 Thess. 5:25; 2 Thess. 3:1). He encouraged the Philippians, "I always pray with joy because of your partnership in the gospel" (Phil. 1:4–5). He prayed for the Colossians too. "Since the day we heard about you, we have not stopped praying for you" (Col. 1:9). And he counseled the Ephesians always to "keep on praying for all the saints" (Eph. 6:18). Praying for others not only brings blessing to them, it brings joy to us.

People in Old Testament times also prayed for others. Some of their requests may seem strange to us, but they were real to them, and they show us the value of praying for others. Recorded in 2 Kings 6 is one of the strangest prayers in the Bible, but one that is entirely for others.

Some neighbors just don't get along, especially in the Middle East. The animosity between Syria and Israel has always run especially deep. In Elisha's day the Syrians engaged in an on-again, off-again war with Israel. Israel's ancient antagonists were not called Syrians at that time but Arameans, sons of Shem, the son of Noah (Gen. 10:22–23).

The Arameans would swoop down on Israel in surprise attacks, destroying crops and occasionally taking prisoners. Then something happened that changed the balance of power. Jehovah began revealing to Elisha the battle plans of the king of Aram. Before his armies could execute their plans, Elisha warned Israel's king so he could take evasive action.

Ben-Hadad, the Aramean king, became extremely frustrated, and when he learned it was Elisha who was tipping off Israel's king, he was enraged. "Go, find out where he is," the king ordered, "so I can send men and capture him" (v. 13).

An intelligence report placed the prophet in Dothan. The Arameans made an overnight march with horses and chariots to surround the city. There was no way Elisha could escape. He didn't stand a prayer, or did he?

The next morning Elisha's servant got up early, and when he looked outside he could hardly believe his eyes. Where there had only been sheep and an occasional shepherd the night before, the dawn's early light revealed a massive Aramean army. Dothan was surrounded. The servant rushed to tell Elisha.

How would the prophet respond to such threatening news? Would he panic? No, he would pray. In fact, he would offer three quick prayers to God—three prayers for others.

PRAYER ONE: OPEN EYES TO FAITH

Elisha's servant asked, "Oh, my lord, what shall we do?" (v. 15). The prophet said, "Don't be afraid" (v. 16). It would be another classic contest between fear and faith.

While fear itself may be the only thing we have to fear, Elisha's servant took a head count and knew there were thousands of reasons to fear that morning. He didn't need something to calm his fears. He needed something to take them away. The only known antidote to fear is faith.

There's an inscription at the Hind's Head Inn in Bray, England, that captures this truth perfectly. It says, "Fear knocked at the door. Faith answered. No one was there!"

Elisha wanted to show his servant there was no reason to fear. Elisha assured his servant, "Those who are with us are more than those who are with them" (v. 16).

The prophet was talking about the unseen host that God provides to protect his people. Psalm 91 assures us when we dwell in the secret place of the Most High God, his angels will guard us in all our ways (Ps. 91:11).

Sometimes we feel a little spooky talking about guardian angels, but God promises us a host of helpers—unseen spirits—who attend to our needs. The writer of Hebrews called them ministering spirits, "sent to serve those who will inherit salvation" (Heb. 1:14). Call them what you want, God says they're there.

But if we live in the presence of an unseen host, we should learn more about them and how they go about their business. Elisha's story fills in some of the details.

God's Hosts Are Not Always Discerned by God's Enemies

Don't tell them, but the enemies of the cross are making a big mistake. Like the king of Aram and his armies, they fail to discern that God has an invisible host, standing near our elbows, ready to intervene in our behalf.

This was the mistake Pharaoh made when he refused to let God's people go. Failure to discern the divine hosts was the mistake Nero made when he attempted to crush the spread of Christianity by killing the early Christians. It was the error Satan made when he planted the seeds of mistrust in the hearts of the Auca warriors who slew five young missionaries.

Underestimating the ability of God has been a consistent mistake of Satan and his stooges. If Ben-Hadad had seen the invisible host of God surrounding Elisha, he never would have sent his forces into battle. And yet, having already lost the war, Satan continues to send detachments of evil angels to menace you and me. It makes good sense to him, but it's a colossal mistake.

God's Hosts Are Not Always Discerned by God's People

But Ben-Hadad was not the only one who didn't see the angels. Elisha's servant didn't see them either. Elisha's servant loved Jehovah. Why else would he travel with Elisha? Yet he didn't see the chariots and horses of heaven. He didn't have eyes of faith.

But hasn't that happened to all of us? How often we see the problems that face us but not the solutions God has provided. Frequently we lack the faith to believe God can overcome any problem we face. We are men and women of faith until the bottom falls out of our business. We are men and women of faith until the biopsy comes back positive. We are men and women of faith until the police come to our door looking for our children. Then our faith turns to questions.

"Why did God let this happen?" "Doesn't God promise that our children will grow up to follow him if we teach them his ways?" "How could God allow cancer to eat away at my body?" While these are legitimate questions, they're not expressions of faith.

An unruly band came to Gethsemane to bind Jesus and take him away. Peter took out his sword and sliced off the ear of the high priest's servant. In telling Peter to put away his sword Jesus said, "Do you think I cannot call on my Father, and he will at once put at my disposal more than twelve legions of angels?" (Matt. 26:53).

Peter should have known that. He had been around awhile—unlike Elisha's servant who was new at his job, having just replaced the greedy Gehazi (see 2 Kings 5:15–27). Maybe his anemic faith can be excused.

But Peter demonstrates that time in the family isn't always the key to discernment—faith is.

God's Hosts Are Always Discerned by Faith

It wasn't Elisha's servant the armies of Aram were after; it was Elisha. Still, Elisha was concerned that his servant see the faithfulness of God. This was the perfect time to teach him. It was also a great time to pray. One of the great prayers of the Bible came as a result of this crisis of faith.

"And Elisha prayed, 'O LORD, open his eyes so he may see.' Then the LORD opened the servant's eyes, and he looked and saw the hills full of horses and chariots of fire all around Elisha" (v. 17).

There is something truly remarkable here. Not angels or horses or chariots. It's Elisha. Notice that he was not at all concerned about himself or his safety. His concern was for others. The prophet wanted his servant to have the kind of faith that sees the invisible, believes the unbelievable, thinks the unthinkable.

What is faith? If you were put on the spot in a Bible study group and asked to define faith, what would you say? Here's my definition: Faith is confidence in the righteous character of God that fosters trust and hope, even when our circumstances foster doubt and despair.

Elisha's circumstances surely would have fostered doubt in God's goodness and despair for his own life. Still, he had faith in God, faith that saw invisible hosts. He prayed that his servant would enjoy that same kind of faith.

One of the prayers I have always prayed for my children is that they would be men and women of faith. In our scientific world, a world where people trust more in themselves than in God, I have prayed that my children would look beyond their circumstances to the righteous character of God. If God has character worth trusting, he has character worth trusting when the bills pile up, when the news from the doctor isn't good, when the enemy launches surprise attacks against us.

In this trilogy of prayers, Elisha first prayed that the Lord would open the eyes of his servant to see the hills full of horses and flaming chariots. God answered that prayer.

Empowered prayer always comes back to faith. Prayer that begins without faith proceeds without power. Faith is a key ingredient in empowered prayer and empowered prayer is a key ingredient in developing the eyes of faith in others.

When you pray for others, pray that God will increase their faith. Pray that he will give your children sight beyond their circumstances. Pray your church will see the host of angels God has prepared to help those who have eyes of faith. Next to praying for someone's salvation, these may be the most empowered prayers you can pray for others.

PRAYER TWO: CLOSE EYES TO REALITY

Elisha's second prayer was also for others, but it was very different from the first. His first prayer was for his servant's eyes to be opened; his second was for his enemy's eyes to be closed.

"As the enemy came down toward him, Elisha prayed to the LORD, 'Strike these people with blindness.' So he struck them with blindness, as Elisha had asked" (v. 18).

Was the blindness of the Aramean soldiers literal blindness? Some think they were just befuddled and didn't know where they were. I believe they were stricken with temporary physical blindness. Either way, when God empowers us to pray, things happen.

Recognize these points about prayer and blindness.

Blindness Was an Act of God

Elisha didn't have a can of mace. The Aramean blindness was the result of one man who was empowered to pray.

This was not the first time God used blindness as both a punishment for wickedness and a demonstration of his grace. Lot's escape from Sodom was facilitated by God temporarily blinding the homosexual men there (Gen. 19:11). This both punished the Sodomites for their wickedness and demonstrated God's grace in saving Lot. What was true of physical blindness is also true of spiritual blindness. God has delivered his chosen people, the Jews, into temporary, spiritual blindness. Jews do not recognize Jesus as Christ the Lord. They have rejected the only Messiah they will ever have. This spiritual blindness was mentioned as early as Deuteronomy 29:2–4.

The sovereign God can use blindness for his divine purposes, whether physical or spiritual. When he chooses to close eyes to reality, nothing can keep them open. But the converse is also true. When God chooses to open blind eyes, either physical or spiritual, nothing can hinder him.

Blindness Was to Benefit Others

It's easy to see why Elisha prayed for the army to be blinded. With the Arameans blinded, the prophet was singlehandedly able to perform an astonishing military victory.

"Elisha told them, 'This is not the road and this is not the city. Follow me, and I will lead you to the man you are looking for.' And he led them to Samaria" (v. 19).

What a sight that must have been. Soldiers muttering to each other, bewildered by their blindness, stumbling over every stick and stone along the road. Samaria was in the hill country; Dothan in the valley. The soldiers must have been a pathetic sight climbing the central hills of Palestine, holding on to each other—the blind leading the blind.

The blindness of these Gentiles benefitted Israel. Ironically, the spiritual blindness of Israel benefitted the Gentiles. God blinded the Jews spiritually so their eyes could not see the truth about Jesus. That opened the door for Gentiles to trust Christ as Savior. The apostle Paul said that spiritual blindness came to God's chosen people so salvation could come to the Gentiles (Rom. 11:11).

If you want to experience God's power in prayer, thank him for the opportunity to trust Christ as Savior. And while you're at it, pray that the scales of spiritual blindness will soon fall from the eyes of your Jewish friends. If their blindness benefitted you, shouldn't your prayers benefit them?

Blindness Was a Prerequisite to Sight

God is not finished with his people Israel. Romans 11 makes it clear that one day the Jews will see the error of rejecting Jesus, and masses of Jewish people will come to their Messiah and Savior. Their blindness not only benefitted the Gentiles, it also was the prerequisite to their spiritual sight.

What was true for the Jews spiritually was true for these Arameans physically. The prophet led them to the city not to kill them but to show them God's amazing grace. The man who prayed God would open the eyes of his servant also prayed God would close the eyes of his enemy. Both prayers were empowered by God. Both were well motivated. Both were for the good of others.

Why did Elisha pray for the Arameans' eyes to be closed? Probably to keep them from false solutions. Without blinded eyes they would have exercised their military might and been slaughtered by God's unseen host. Elisha did not pray for their destruction; he prayed for their deliverance.

When empowered to pray for others, we should keep two things in mind. First, we must have the same pure motivation the prophet had. Elisha was not vindictive in his prayer, and neither should we be. Empowered prayer does not spring from improper motivation.

Second, we must be mindful of the program of God. Blindness precedes sight. Your friends and family without Christ are spiritually blind, but that's why you pray for them. Pray they will not blindly trust the false solutions handed to them by the world. Pray God will put in them a desire for spiritual sight. Pray their blindness will last only until someone can lead them to the city of sight. That's being empowered to pray for others.

PRAYER THREE: OPEN EYES TO SALVATION

The third of Elisha's one-sentence prayers was offered as soon as this curious retinue entered Samaria. Elisha had twice prayed for others. One prayer was for eyes to be opened; the second was for eyes to be closed. Now he again prays for eyes to be opened.

"After they entered the city, Elisha said, 'LORD, open the eyes of these men so they can see.' Then the LORD opened their eyes and they looked, and there they were, inside Samaria" (v. 20).

For the Aramean armies, their worst nightmare was not being blinded. Their worst nightmare was opening their eyes and discovering they were standing inside Israel's capital city. That's a real ego deflator.

When the enemy opened their eyes, the king of Israel spoke first. He asked Elisha, "Shall I kill them, my father? Shall I kill them?" (v. 21). (Apparently the king called the prophet father as a term of respect.)

The Israelite king was almost giddy with excitement. These Arameans had menaced him for years. Suddenly the shoe was on the other foot. They were completely at his mercy. It was too good to be true.

The Israelites were in the habit of putting to death their prisoners of war (1 Sam. 15:8). The law permitted it (Deut. 20:13). King Joram was anxious to administer justice. But not this day. It was not God's plan. Jehovah didn't want to kill the Arameans; he wanted to save the prophet from being killed.

Elisha said, "Set food and water before them so that they may eat and drink and then go back to their master" (v. 22).

Israel's enemy would not be put to death. In fact, Israel's king fed them sumptuously, not a little snack but a great feast. After they finished, he sent them back to their homeland.

THREE OBSERVATIONS

Several things about Elisha's three prayers stand out like halogen headlights on high beam.

First, all three were sentence prayers. They were not elaborate. They do not display the A-C-T-S formula of longer prayers. Not all prayers do. But they are beautiful in their simplicity: "Open his eyes so he may see." "Strike these people with blindness." "Open the eyes of these men so they can see." That's getting down to business.

What is more impressive, however, is Elisha spoke each of these prayers in the context of great faith. Elisha was surrounded by enemy soldiers, but he saw only God's hosts. His circumstances fostered doubt and despair, but his faith fostered trust and hope in God. Prayers of faith are always empowered by God.

But the most impressive thing about Elisha's three quick prayers is that each one was in behalf of someone else. Not one contained a first person pronoun. Elisha never mentioned himself in his three prayers. His prayers were entirely for others.

It says something about our Christian character and maturity when we can pray—not once or twice but three times—and never mention ourselves. God wants us to pray about our needs and desires, but not exclusively about our needs and desires.

When you pray, do you ever come up short on material? Do your prayers last two or three minutes on average? Maybe you're short of power and material because you're short of interest in others.

When you pray for others, you open yourself to a whole new world of joy in prayer. Don't miss the joy. Focus less inward, more outward, and always upward. You may be shocked at what you've been missing.

Grandparents, you especially are on the threshold of increased joy. When those little grandchildren were born, more than toys and tots settled into your life. Pray for them every day. Pray for the blindness of sin to fall early from their eyes. Pray for a committed life to the Lord. Pray for them to be men and women of faith. God gave *us* grandchildren; he gave *them* people empowered to pray. What a deal!

Don't neglect an empowered prayer life for others.

ON-LINE PRAYER

What does it mean to be empowered to pray? It means showcasing the needs of others in your petitions.

Charles Delucena Meigs wrote:

> Lord, help me live from day to day
> In such a self-forgetful way,
> That even when I kneel to pray,
> My prayer shall be for others.

Take some time today to pray wholly for other people—your friends, your relatives, your neighbors, those at work, those you meet on vacation. Pray for each of them to have eyes of faith. Pray for them to be blind to the false solutions of the world. And pray that all who are yet outside of God's family will see salvation by the grace of God. Ask God to empower you to pray for others. They'll never be the same; neither will you!

Father in heaven, we praise you for including us in your great love. Thank you for reaching out to us. Now Lord, there are others in our lives who need you. They are blinded by the world—its values, its thinking, its solutions to their problems. Keep us from being selfish. Keep us from praying only for ourselves and our needs. Help us to be faithful to others by constantly bringing them to your attention. Thank you for this privilege, Father. Accept our thanks in Jesus' name. Amen.

Part 3

LEARNING HOW

8 What's Important in Prayer

Jonah's Prayer
Jonah 2:1–10

Being empowered to pray
means enjoying a right relationship with God.

Been to the grocery store lately? What an experience! Aisles and aisles of things I don't want. Do you think they purposely make it difficult to get to the back of the store?

There are several things I can't figure out about grocery stores. For instance, what deeper intelligence decides where to place things in the store? Why is the milk so far from the entrance? When I pop into the store for a half gallon of milk, do they really think I'm going to buy all that stuff on the way to the dairy case?

Wouldn't it make sense to put the bread alongside the peanut butter and jelly? And can't they group cereals, putting all the cereals with prizes in one section so kids can go right for them and the bran cereals in another section so their grandparents can go right for them? Doesn't that make sense? Why must we wade through all those things unimportant to us just to discover those few things that are?

Churches are sometimes like supermarkets. Christians sometimes argue over things that don't matter. Church members have come to blows over whether to use plastic or glass communion cups. The color of choir robes is so important that new churches have been planted in order to settle the issue.

It seems the less important the issue, the more time we spend discussing it. This even happens when the topic is prayer. Prayer issues that are of least importance have the most books and articles written about them.

The prayer of Jonah in the belly of the great fish perfectly illustrates the underwhelming importance of some issues. We can learn major lessons about prayer from this minor prophet.

THE PRAYER OF THE PROPHET

After a graphic description of what it was like in the belly of a fish, the prophet said, "When my life was ebbing away, I remembered you, LORD, and my prayer rose to you" (Jonah 2:7).

Jonah prayed and God answered. Many of the things that people feel bring power in prayer are missing from Jonah's prayer. Let's see what's not important to God when we pray.

Who We Are

Jonah was God's prophet to Israel in the days of King Jeroboam (2 Kings 14:23–25). We know next to nothing about him, except he was the son of Amittai and from the village of Gath Hepher (2 Kings 14:25). Surely God did not hear Jonah's prayer because of his importance.

Called to go to Nineveh—the hated enemy of the Jews—Jonah instead went down to the port of Joppa. He boarded a ship that would take him the opposite direction, to Tarshish, about 2,500 miles west of Joppa and as far from Nineveh and God's call as Jonah could get.

Is this the kind of person who gets his prayers answered? Yes, in fact, it is, because who you are is not God's criteria for being empowered to pray.

Prayer is not the privilege of the spiritual elite. It's not reserved for a special few. Prayer is not for perfect people. If it were, none of us would be empowered. Anyone who has access to God through the blood of Jesus Christ can pray (Rom. 5:1–2). Prayer is for people who have a need and a relationship with God that can fill that need. Prayer is for couples in debt. Prayer is for grandmothers who are alone. Prayer is for teenagers seeking God's will. Prayer is for corporate officers pondering a new business venture. Prayer is for all of us.

Think about the kinds of people who pray. They're as varied as the thirty-one flavors of Baskin Robbins.

Moses was a chided, unappreciated leader. The people he led criticized him mercilessly. Still, when he prayed for victory over the Amalekites, God answered his prayer, and victory was won (Exod. 17).

Hannah was a bitter, childless wife. Her rival succeeded in making Hannah's life miserable. Hannah cried out to God for a son, and God answered her prayer (1 Sam. 1).

The early Christians were a disorganized, motley group, desperately in need of leadership. Peter was the obvious choice, but he soon suffered the frequent fate of those in frontline leadership: He was imprisoned. The disorganized church organized a prayer meeting, and God answered their prayers. Peter escaped from prison unharmed (Acts 12).

Paul and Silas were an overworked, underpaid duet on the Midnight Special, singing their songs from a Philippian cell. But when they prayed, God answered their prayers, and the dungeon doors flew open (Acts 16).

Julie, a third-grader, had a friend who cut her finger during recess. As the teacher took the friend to the nurse for a Band-Aid, Julie prayed that God would make her friend feel better. Her prayer was answered.

Bob was a Sunday school teacher who felt very inadequate for the task. He prayed that God would give him patience with his junior high boys. He prayed they would ask sharp questions that would enhance their learning. And he prayed that his life would teach the boys as much as his lessons did. His prayers were answered too.

Do these examples have any similarities? We see both men and women, Old Testament, New Testament, and contemporary settings, old and young people. The common denominator is they were empowered to pray, and God answered their prayers.

Who they were was unimportant. Their position in life was of no consequence. God did not answer their prayers because of who they were. What was important was their relationship with God.

Jonah was a prophet, but that didn't *cause* God to answer his prayer. He was a disobedient prophet, but that didn't *keep* God from answering his prayer. Because when he prayed, Jonah was a repentant prophet.

If you think prayer is only for the saintly elders of the church or for those who have fallen deeply into sin, you're shopping in the wrong aisles. Keep on moving. The good stuff is yet to come.

Where We Are

We pray in many places: in church, in our cars, in airplanes. Most of us have prayed just about everywhere.

The house of God is the premier house of prayer. When Jesus entered the temple area and encountered men carrying on commerce in the temple courts, he chided these merchants and drove them out of the temple: "'My house will be called a house of prayer,' but you are making it a 'den of robbers'" (Matt. 21:13).

We go to church to worship God, to learn of him, to fellowship with others who love him, to pray. The serenity of the church makes a conducive atmosphere for prayer. But Jesus himself did not reserve prayer for the temple. While God's house may be a special place to pray, it's not the only place to pray.

Where we pray is not the secret to empowerment. God's people have prayed everywhere.

Paul prayed in the temple (Acts 21, 22), but he also prayed in prison (Acts 16). He prayed on the seashore (Acts 21). Apparently the apostle felt anyplace was an appropriate place for prayer.

Acts 10 records the prayers of Cornelius and Peter. Acts 10:2 says of Cornelius, "He and all his family were devout and God-fearing; he gave generously to those in need and prayed to God regularly." Presumably Cornelius prayed in his house. On the other hand Peter "went up on the roof to pray" (v. 9).

Think of all the places Jesus prayed. After feeding the five thousand, Jesus went to one of the hills rising from the Sea of Galilee to pray (Matt. 14:23). He also prayed at Caesarea Philippi at the foothills of Mount Hermon, where Peter confessed him as the Christ (Luke 9:18). And he prayed on the Mount of Transfiguration (Luke 9:28).

Jesus was fond of going to the hills to pray (Mark 6:46). He prayed at the Jordan River when he was baptized (Luke 3:21). He prayed in the wilderness, in lonely places (Luke 5:16). He prayed for his disciples in the upper room (John 17), and he prayed in agony at Gethsemane's garden (Matt. 26:36).

Jesus called the temple a house of prayer, but he prayed anywhere and everywhere. It's not the place that empowers you to pray. You can pray anywhere—and should.

Our Position

The great prayers of the Bible reveal that people prayed in all kinds of positions. Take this little prayer quiz. (Answers are on page 132.)

1. What position was Daniel in when he prayed before his open window?
2. What position did Moses assume when he prayed for rebellious Israel?
3. What position did Christ choose for prayer?

Jesus prayed in many different positions. Position is not the point.

Have you ever wondered what position Jonah was in when he prayed? There he was in the belly of the great fish, covered with seaweed and being pickled by gastric juices. Somehow I can't imagine Jonah being concerned about his prayer position in the fish's belly. It wasn't important to him; it shouldn't be to us either.

I wish I knew who wrote the following poem. It so wonderfully expresses what our attitudes should be toward our position in prayer.

"The proper way for man to pray," said Deacon Lemuel
   Keyes,
"the only proper attitude is down upon one's knees."
"Nay, I should say the way to pray," said Reverend Doctor
   Wise,
"is standing straight with outstretched arms with rapt and
   upturned eyes."
"Oh no, no, no," said Elder Snow, "such posture is too
   proud.
A man should pray with eyes fast-closed and head con-
   tritely bowed."
"It seems to me his hands should be austerely clasped in
   front,
with both thumbs pointing to the ground," said Reverend
   Doctor Blunt.
"Last year I fell in Hodgkin's well, headfirst," said Cyril
   Brown,
"with both my heels a-stickin' up, my head a-pointin' down.
And I done prayed right then and there, best prayer I ever
   said,
   the prayin'est prayer I ever prayed, a-standin' on my head."

Is it important we learn the secret of empowered prayer?
Yes it is. Is the position we assume in prayer the secret? Not
on your life. Who we are is not important. Where we are is
not important. What position we assume is not important.

What time we pray is not important. Jesus prayed all
night (Luke 6:12) as well as in the morning (Mark 1:35).
Whether we pray alone, with a few friends, or in a crowd
is not important. Jesus prayed with his twelve disciples
(Luke 9:18), with Peter, James, and John (Luke 9:28),
and alone (Luke 22:41).

So what is truly important in prayer? What empowers
us to pray? I thought you'd never ask!

Our Relationship

Jonah was an unfaithful prophet who ran from God, thereby breaking his fellowship with the Father. But after the great fish swallowed him, Jonah began to sense his deep need for God. By running from God's will Jonah was also running from God's blessing. Whether he was praying on his knees or while doing the dog paddle in the fish's belly was unimportant. What was important was he came to grips with his sin, repented, and sought a right relationship with God.

The key element in getting our prayers answered is our relationship with God. That's where empowerment begins.

What is your relationship with God? Paul said, "There is one God and one mediator between God and men, the man Christ Jesus" (1 Tim. 2:5). We were estranged from God because of our sin. But Christ's death on Calvary's cross satisfied God's requirement for atonement, and it made a way for us to have a relationship with God. If we receive Christ into our life, his blood washes away our sins. That same blood gives us access to God through prayer. Paul reminded the Roman Christians that it was through the Lord Jesus that we have access to the Father (Rom. 5:2).

Jesus died to change your relationship with God from stranger to son. But even now that relationship is constantly being strained. So he intercedes with the Father to repair your relationship when it is damaged by sin (Heb. 7:25–26).

The key is relationship. If your relationship with God is built on faith in Jesus Christ as Lord and Savior, you have discovered what is truly important in prayer. There is no empowerment to pray without a right relationship with God. And there is no access to the Father without a relationship with Jesus.

Praying in Jesus' name is not just a tag we put on the end of our prayers. Praying in Jesus' name means we have discovered the secret of getting through to God. We are empowered to pray by the benefits of the Son's death and resurrection. We pray to the Father only through the power of what his Son did for us at Calvary.

ON-LINE PRAYER

God is not impressed with who we are, for *in Christ* we are heirs of God (Rom. 8:17). God is not impressed with where we are, for *in Christ* we are never separated from the Father (Rom. 8:38–39). God is not impressed with what position we assume, for we have an exalted position *in Christ* (Rom. 8:32–33). The only thing that impresses God is that we are *in Christ*. That's where the power is.

So if you're looking to be empowered to pray through external things, you're looking in the wrong aisle. Move on to the important things. Move on to a right relationship with God. That's what's truly important in prayer.

Dear loving Father, you have gone to great lengths to establish a relationship with us. You did it at the expense of your Son's life. Thank you, Father, for giving the best you had to create a right relationship with us. And yet, Lord, there are times our relationship with you becomes clouded by our own sin. We know it can never be severed; nothing can separate us from the love of God in Christ Jesus. But we don't want our relationship with you to suffer from our own selfish sin. Forgive us, Father, and renew a right spirit within us. To this end we pray in the name of Jesus. Amen.

Answers to quiz:

1. "Three times a day he got down on his knees and prayed, giving thanks to his God" (Dan. 6:10).
2. "I lay prostrate before the LORD those forty days and forty nights because the LORD had said he would destroy you. I prayed to the LORD and said, 'O Sovereign LORD, do not destroy your people'" (Deut. 9:25–26).
3. At his baptism he prayed standing in the water (Luke 3:21). Reclining at the triclinium table in the upper room, he delivered a discourse and then prayed for his disciples (John 17). In the Garden of Gethsemane Jesus "fell with his face to the ground and prayed" (Matt. 26:39).

    Yet when Jesus finished praying and returned to find his disciples sleeping, he said, "Get up and pray so that you will not fall into temptation" (Luke 22:46).

Make Prayer a Habit

9

Hezekiah's Prayer
2 Kings 19:14–19, 35–37

Being empowered to pray means being so much in the habit of prayer that when you need to pray, you don't need to discuss it.

Alaska is a land of incredible beauty. Much of the state is unspoiled wilderness. A fisherman's and photographer's paradise, it's the only state of the fifty United States where you are as apt to fly as to drive.

I once spoke in Alaska at a pastors conference. When my wife and I arrived at the Anchorage International Airport, a missionary friend flew us to the tiny fishing village of Seldovia on the Kenai Peninsula. We spent the night in a bed-and-breakfast perched on the rocks above the Cook Inlet.

In the morning we took off from Seldovia's gravel runway and climbed up the western edge of the Kenai Mountains. Our flight plan called for us to fly over the mountains, along the Kenai fjords toward Valdez, and then north to the Gulkana airport. We climbed to 11,000 feet and began crossing the mountains. They were snow-covered and breathtaking. We had just flown over the first peaks, however, when we encountered moderate turbulence. It began to snow. Visibility decreased. Turbulence grew worse. Our six seater Cessna began to rock and roll.

The pilot, Dwayne King, chief missionary pilot for SEND International, has more than twenty-five years flying experience in Alaska. When the turbulence continued to increase, he banked left and flew away from the mountain range. He looked at me in the seat next to him and said, "It's too bumpy. We're not going to cross here today. We'll fly along the mountains and cross at the Matanuska Glacier." We all breathed a sigh of relief. An hour later we landed safely at Gulkana. Wisdom had prevailed.

There were five of us in the plane that day, and we all benefited from our pilot's experience. He knew when it was safe to tackle the turbulence and when it was wise to wing our way elsewhere. Before you get into a threatening situation, it's good to know what you should do. That comes from experience.

What's true for flying is also true for praying. When you are under attack from Satan, that's not the time to learn how to pray. Learn how to pray before you encounter desperate situations in life.

THE INFLUENCE OF A GOOD KING

Hezekiah knew what to do before trouble came. He was one of the good kings of Judah, a man of prayer. In fact, so inspirational is the story of Hezekiah's prayer that it's recorded in three Old Testament books: 2 Kings 19, 2 Chronicles 32, and Isaiah 37.

Hezekiah's father, Ahaz, had not been a good example to him. Ahaz reigned sixteen years in Jerusalem and followed "the detestable ways of the nations the LORD had driven out before the Israelites" (2 Kings 16:3). But Hezekiah was different. He determined to undo the damage done by his wicked father. The list of his reforms is remarkable. Hezekiah removed the high places, smashed the sacred stones, and cut down the sacred groves devoted to the worship of Asherah.

Hezekiah ranks right up there with Luther, Calvin, and the great reformers of history. But he didn't just rid Judah of paganism; he had a positive agenda as well. Hezekiah trusted Jehovah, the God of Israel. In fact, 2 Kings 18:5 says, "There was no one like him among all the kings of Judah, either before him or after him." That's quite a compliment!

One godly leader in a position of influence can make a significant difference in the direction of an entire nation.

But there was trouble in Judah.

THE ATTACK OF A GODLESS KING

Judah was protected by a series of strategically located fortress cities. The Assyrian armies moved into southern Palestine and systematically attacked fortress after fortress. Sennacherib sent three of his field lieutenants to Jerusalem with an ultimatum. They shouted invectives over the city wall, blaspheming God and belittling Hezekiah.

When King Hezekiah heard what the Assyrians were saying, he tore his clothes, put on sackcloth, and went into the temple to pray. He informed the prophet Isaiah of the situation, who then relayed this message from God: "Do not be afraid of what you have heard . . . I am going to put such a spirit in him [Sennacherib] that when he hears a certain report, he will return to his own country, and there I will have him cut down with the sword" (2 Kings 19:6–7). Sennacherib again sent messengers to Jerusalem promising the complete destruction of the city and its inhabitants. The stage was set for a classic confrontation.

THE PRAYER OF A HELPLESS KING

The greatest threat to Hezekiah's reign was outside Jerusalem's walls promising to crash the gates. What would Hezekiah do against such a formidable enemy? What the king did was pray one of the most instructive prayers in the Bible. We learn more about how to pray from this prayer than from any other in the Old Testament.

Let's investigate what makes this one of the great prayers of the Bible.

Instinctively Spontaneous

Was this the first time Hezekiah ever prayed? Not a chance. His actions reflect his experience. He was in the habit of taking everything to God in prayer, which is why this prayer was instinctively spontaneous.

The king never considered doing anything else. There was only one answer to their problem. If Jehovah didn't save Judah, no one else could! It was spontaneous because the king called no advisors, formed no committees, consulted with none of the Joint Chiefs of Staff. He skipped all that and went right to God.

Are you instinctive when you pray? Is taking your need to God the first thing that comes to your mind, or does

God rank further down on your list of potential solutions (the "if all else fails, try prayer" approach)?

In 1981 I bought my first car with a computerized control panel. On the dash was a panel of lights. Whenever anything went wrong with the car, a light would come on to indicate the problem. After having this car a few weeks, I was driving on a country road near Portland, Maine, when a dashboard light came on saying, "Check Engine." I was puzzled. I pulled off the road, got out of the car, lifted the hood, and sure enough—the engine was in there. Check engine. What does that mean?

A short time later my wife and I were driving south on Interstate 81 through Pennsylvania. It was a Saturday night and I was to preach in Chambersburg, Pennsylvania, the next morning. Suddenly a light on my dash said, "Charge." What did that mean? I was going as fast as the law allowed! Again I pulled off the road. I soon concluded that the alternator was not working properly. We had to find a garage.

Linda and I instinctively began to pray. We left the interstate and drove through town after town, all with gas stations—all closed.

As we left one tiny town, I saw an Exxon station and pulled off the road to see if it was closed. Sure enough, it was. Then my wife said, "Why don't you ask him where there may be an open station?" I looked to my left, and there, standing in the doorway of a small house, was a man looking back at me.

I got out of the car, went up to the man, and told him my problem. "Are there any gas stations open around here?" I asked.

"Nope. None open now. It's after six o'clock," he replied.

I thanked him and returned to the car. He followed me and asked, "What do you need?"

"I think I need a belt for my alternator."

"Nope. You'll never find a belt at this hour."

Again I thanked him and got into the car. He knocked on my window. "What size belt do you need?"

I began to wonder if he was just inquisitive or intent on torturing me. I said, "I don't know, but it fits this car."

Then the man said, "Wait here. If you'll be patient, maybe I can help you." He disappeared back into the house.

We waited a few minutes. Suddenly a huge garage door opened at the building adjacent to the man's house. He stood in the doorway, motioning for me to come to him. I got out of the car, walked into the huge garage, and there—conservatively speaking—were one million fan belts. It had to be the fan belt hall of fame. There were more belts than I had ever seen before, hanging everywhere. They were used, however, and not sized. The man took a long pole, got down a couple of belts, and found one that fit my engine. I paid him, thanked God and my stoic friend, and soon we were on our way.

Do you think we just happened to stop in front of the world's largest collection of belts? Not for a minute. We were supernaturally directed by God. We had prayed instinctively, spontaneously, and the Lord answered our prayer in a most dramatic way.

When you need empowerment for prayer, that's not the time to learn how to pray. Be like Hezekiah. Get into the habit of taking everything to God in prayer. Whatever you need. Big or little. Be instinctive; be spontaneous. "O what peace we often forfeit, O what needless pain we bear, all because we do not carry everything to God in prayer!" (Joseph Scriven).

Praisefully Reverent

Hezekiah's prayer began with a quality so often missing in our prayers today. He began with reverent praise to God. He lifted up Jehovah's name. "O LORD, God of Israel, enthroned between the cherubim, you alone are God over all the kingdoms of the earth. You have made heaven and earth" (2 Kings 19:15).

Are your prayers reverent? In our irreverent society, what does it mean to revere God?

The word *reverent* (Hebrew, *yare*) literally means to fear. In the moral sense it means to revere. It's not the kind of fear we have of the dark; it's the kind of reverence we have for electricity. We are awed by electricity's power. We don't fully understand it, and so we have a healthy reverence for it.

The same is true with God. He is awesome, not totally comprehendible, and therefore to be revered.

This Hebrew word is used in Genesis 28:17 where Jacob awakened from his ladder dream and said, "How awesome is this place! This is none other than the house of God; this is the gate of heaven."

When we begin praying by expressing our reverence for God, it tells him something about us. It tells him we recognize who he is and who we are. He is worthy; we are unworthy. He is uncommon; we are common. He is to be revered; we are to revere him.

The initial words of Hezekiah's prayer distinguished Jehovah from all other gods. He prayed to Jehovah, the God of Israel, "enthroned between the cherubim" (2 Kings 19:15). Of all the deities of the ancient Near East, only Jehovah resided between the cherubim. Of course today we speak to God in the authority of Jesus' name (Eph. 5:20; Heb. 13:15). We no longer have the ark of the covenant, nor do we need it. If some Indiana

Jones type one day discovers the ark, it will be of little consequence. When you have the Lord Jesus, who needs an ark?

If you want to be empowered to pray, follow Hezekiah's pattern. Begin your prayers by showing God you believe he is someone wise enough, holy enough, powerful enough to pray to. Give some thought to how you will extol the person and name of God. Make your prayers praisefully reverent. Tell him right up front that you revere him.

Intimately Personal

Reverence for God doesn't mean distance from him. Do you talk to God as if he were far away? Do you envision God as a kindly grandfather sitting on an exalted throne way off in space? Or do you speak to him as if he were right there in the room with you? How personal are you when you pray to God?

Hezekiah was intimately personal. He prayed, "Give ear, O LORD, and hear; open your eyes, O LORD, and see; listen to the words Sennacherib has sent to insult the living God" (2 Kings 19:16).

It's as though Hezekiah were asking God to bend down, put his ear close to Hezekiah's mouth, and listen. That's personal.

I enjoy being a grandfather. I love holding the little hands of my grandchildren (after they've been "destickified"). I treasure those little laughs and giggles. Little children are not as strong as big fathers or grandfathers, but you'd never know it. When my grandchildren pull down on my finger, they demonstrate that the finger bone is connected to the hand bone, and the hand bone is connected to the arm bone, and the arm bone is connected to the shoulder bone. When they pull down on my finger, they get a whole grandfather. I bend over to hear what they're saying, even though I don't need to be that close.

That's the way it is with God. He wants us to be intimately personal with him. Ask him to bend down from heaven and place his ear right where you can speak directly into it, and he'll do it. He's that kind of God.

The next time you pray, don't treat God as if he were some impersonal force. Don't approach him as some distant deity. Approach him personally, intimately. Approach him as your Abba, Father. Learn the delicate balance between reverence and intimacy. You can revere God and at the same time speak to him as a father.

Respectfully Informative

Hezekiah prayed, "It is true, O LORD, that the Assyrian kings have laid waste these nations and their lands. They have thrown their gods into the fire and destroyed them, for they were not gods but only wood and stone, fashioned by men's hands" (2 Kings 19:17–18). Hezekiah's prayer was respectfully informative.

God is a remarkable being. He is omnipresent, yet as personal as if he were yours and yours alone. He is immense, yet small enough to fill your tender heart. He is all wise and knows everything perfectly, yet invites you to tell him what's on your mind.

Doesn't God already know what's on your mind? Absolutely. Doesn't he know the desperation of your situation before you tell him? Certainly. Still, God wants you to tell him.

When you ask God to help you stretch your family budget, maybe your prayer goes something like this:

"Dear God, you already know how short of money I'm going to be this month, so there's no sense in my telling you. I need a miracle, Lord. Amen."

God deals in specifics, and when you pray, he wants you to pray in specifics. Tell him exactly what your problem is. Tell him where it hurts, how long it has hurt, and who made it hurt. Tell him how much you're short this month and why. Tell him which child is sick, what you've done to care for him or her, what has worked and what has not. God already knows; still, he delights in your informing him in a respectful manner.

Why? God doesn't want you to tell him so *he* knows how desperate your situation is but so you demonstrate that *you* know how desperate it is. He wants you to tell him your needs in faith and dependence.

So go ahead and tell God what's wrong. He's waiting to hear from you. Tell him all the little details just as you would tell your best friend. Such dependence proves you trust him and really do need him.

Purposefully Direct

Have you heard prayers that seemed to beat around the bush? So has God. Sometimes after I pray, I can almost picture God scratching his head and saying, "I wonder what that was all about?"

While we begin with worship and praise to God, at some point we have to get around to mentioning our specific need. That's when our prayer becomes purposefully direct, as was Hezekiah's.

The king finally got around to saying, "Now, O LORD our God, deliver us from his hand" (v. 19). That's his request. Even though it was urgent, he had framed it with words of worship. At the appropriate time Hezekiah told God exactly what was on his mind.

There's a time and place for everything. It's important to pray for missionaries. Pray for them consistently, by name, by location, by need. But if you're driving down the highway on a winter day with ice on the road, and you notice your car is not exactly oriented the same way as the highway, that's not the time to pull out your missionary list. That's the time to be purposefully direct. "Lord, save me."

Let's not make God scratch his head trying to figure out what our prayers are about. Let's spell out our requests to him specifically. When you pray, pray as Hezekiah did: purposefully direct.

Properly Motivated

Now, this may hurt a little. What is your motivation for praying to God? Is it greed? Do you want more, and you've learned only God can provide it?

It is easy to discern the Pharisee's motivation for prayer in Luke 18:11–12. He wanted to be seen of men and to impress God. But God wasn't impressed.

It is also easy to see Hezekiah's motivation. "Now, O LORD our God, deliver us from his hand, so that all kingdoms on earth may know that you alone, O LORD, are God" (v. 19).

Hezekiah's concern was not for his place in history. His motivation was not to keep from being remembered as the loser king, defeated by Sennacherib. He didn't pray just to save his neck, although there's nothing wrong with that. He prayed that God would be glorified in sparing Jerusalem. Hezekiah's concern was that when God answered his prayer, the whole world would know Jehovah was mighty in behalf of his people.

If you want to be empowered to pray, check your motivation. When you pray for good health, pray to be healthy so you can be of service to God. When you pray for God to meet your financial needs, pray that God's remarkable supply will bring others to trust him. Pray with the highest of all motives—that God will be praised—and you will see new life breathed into your old prayers. You'll see power you only dreamed of before.

That leads me to one final observation about Hezekiah's great prayer.

Powerfully Effective

Do you get answers to your prayers? Hezekiah did. He prayed for God's will in God's way. His prayer was powerfully effective. Verses 21–34 record Isaiah's message from God to Hezekiah. Then verse 35 says, "That night the angel of the LORD went out and put to death 185,000 men in the Assyrian camp. When the people got up the next morning—there were all the dead bodies."

Think about it. Sennacherib had the most powerful army in the world. He had been successful in overrunning every Judean outpost. His massive army surrounded Jerusalem. It appeared as if the die was cast, and Jerusalem would fall.

Likely that would have happened too, except for the prayer of one godly man. No troops were mustered. Not a shot was fired. The people never left the safety of Jerusalem's walls. God did it all. When the Jerusalemites got up the next morning, they discovered 185,000 Assyrian corpses. What a sight! The mighty Assyrian army was dead. God was alive and at work in Israel's behalf, and all as a result of one man's prayer.

Does prayer work? You'll never convince Hezekiah otherwise. Prayer is a powerfully effective tool against Satan and his henchmen. But prayer must be empowered by God if it's going to work.

When you pray in a manner acceptable to God, you'll see results attributable only to God. It pays to know how to pray, to have experience in praying before severe adversity comes. After all, trouble is on the way. You'd better know how to pray before it arrives.

One postscript to this story. When the king's men told Isaiah that Jerusalem was surrounded and about to be destroyed, he said not to worry. He predicted Sennacherib would return to his country and there be killed.

At the time everyone must have thought Isaiah was crazy. They must have laughed behind his back. Well, now that Hezekiah's prayer has been answered and 185,000 Assyrians are dead, read the last two verses of the chapter. Sennacherib returned to Nineveh and was killed by his own sons.

Amazing? Not at all. Hezekiah had prayed an empowered prayer, and such prayers are powerfully effective. God rewards those who cast their cares on him.

Like Hezekiah you can be empowered to pray. Seek God's power as the king did, and then watch God work. Trouble is ahead, but so is the power of prayer.

ON-LINE PRAYER

What does it mean to be empowered to pray? It means being so much in the habit of prayer that when you need to pray, you don't need to discuss it.

Anyone can pray, but significant prayer, like anything else done with real power, comes with practice. The more we're in the habit of praying, the more we become empowered to pray.

Knowing how to pray is important. We wouldn't see the A-C-T-S formula so frequently if it wasn't. Praying spontaneously is also important. But praying spontaneously with the A-C-T-S formula reveals someone who is in the habit of powerful prayer. When you can instinctively pray to God and still be reverent to his name and specific with your requests, you know you're in the habit of empowered prayer. That's experience money can't buy—empowered experience.

> *O Lord, God of Israel, enthroned between the cherubim, you alone are God over all the kingdoms of the earth. You have made heaven and earth. Please listen, O Lord, and hear; please open your eyes, O Lord, and see. We come to you as if it were our first time, fresh and anxious. And yet we come to you as we have done so many times before, experienced and excited. Thank you, Father, for bending your ear to hear us. Lord, expel from us all selfishness and self-desire. Answer our prayer in such a way that the whole world, and especially our immediate friends, will know that you are our God. In the strength of Jesus' name we pray. Amen.*

10 Follow the Leader

Jesus' Prayer
Matthew 6:9–13

Being empowered to pray means praying in the pattern the Lord provided.

The Lord's Prayer.

These three words bring to mind piety and liturgy. Some churches repeat the Lord's Prayer every Sunday morning, occasionally with no thought or little meaning. Others are so afraid of liturgy they wouldn't repeat it if the Lord himself asked them to.

What is it about the Lord's Prayer? It's not magical, and yet it seems almost mystical. It's nothing more than a pattern for prayer, but it rolls off the tongue in poetic beauty. It's unquestionably the premier prayer of the Bible.

Much of our Lord's life was spent in prayer. For instance, after a miracle-packed day of healing and driving out demons, early the next morning Jesus slipped off to a solitary place to pray (Mark 1:35). He really knew how to start a day.

On another occasion Jesus had no sooner fed five thousand people than he dismissed the crowd and "went up on a mountainside by himself to pray" (Matt. 14:23). He really knew how to relax.

Once during a busy day of teaching, some parents brought their children to Jesus to place his hands on them and pray for them. The disciples rebuked the parents, but Jesus prayed for the little ones anyway (Matt. 19:13). He was never too busy to pray.

For Jesus, prayer was as natural as breathing. He was constantly in prayer. But on one occasion when Jesus had finished praying, his disciples said to him, "Lord, teach us to pray" (Luke 11:1). The result was what we commonly call the Lord's Prayer.

Ironically, though Jesus spent much time in prayer, the Lord's Prayer is not a prayer that Jesus could have prayed. How could Jesus say, "Forgive us our debts"? Jesus was in debt to no one; we are all in debt to him. Jesus prayed this great prayer as a pattern for his disciples to follow. It came in response to their desire to be empowered to pray.

It was Wednesday night, prayer meeting night. We had just sung a couple of hymns and listened to a Bible study. The pastor said, "It's time to pray. Turn around, face each other in groups of three or four, and pray for those people listed on your prayer sheet."

Sitting directly in front of me was a large man. His hair was silver gray, and he looked distinguished. John turned around and joined the group I was in. Before we prayed, John looked at me and said, "I'm not very good at this. I mean, I'm not good with words. I don't pray very well." He was embarrassed to pray with the rest of us "professionals."

Wanting to ease John's pain, I said, "None of us is very good at this; some have just had more practice. Let's do what the Lord told us to do in the Lord's Prayer. Let's just thank God for who he is and what he's done for us, and then talk to him about one or two people on our prayer sheet. I'll go first."

We prayed around the circle in a down-home way. When it was John's turn, he joined in. He was right; he wasn't good with words. But he had heart, and his prayer was eloquent in the ears of God.

Later John thanked me for putting him at ease. I told him if he simply followed the pattern of the Lord's Prayer, he wouldn't go wrong. And neither will you. After all, if you're going to learn how to pray, you might as well follow the Leader. Let's learn to pray from someone who really knew how.

If we examine Matthew 6 closely, we'll see the biblical guidelines on how to pray even before the Lord's Prayer begins. The verses leading up to this prayer are filled with tips on how to be empowered to pray. Let's take note of several.

PRAY SINCERELY

The Master Teacher began his class on prayer by saying the following: "And when you pray, do not be like the hypocrites, for they love to pray standing in the synagogues and on the street corners to be seen by men. I tell you the truth, they have received their reward in full" (Matt. 6:5).

Before any other lesson about prayer, we must learn the sincerity lesson. There is no empowerment without sincerity.

Have you ever met a hypocrite? That's like asking if you've ever taken a deep breath. Hypocrites are as plentiful as fleas on a barnyard cat. The word Jesus used for hypocrite is one used of actors on a stage. It means to impersonate, simulate, or pretend. A simple definition of a hypocrite is someone who's not what he appears to be. It's a person who's not himself on Sunday.

That was certainly true of the Pharisees. They loved to stand on the street corners underneath the torch so they would easily be seen by all passersby. There they would pray with great fanfare, using big words and trite expressions. They were praying to impress the people who looked on. They were putting on an act, like players on a stage.

You may know people who are impressive in the way they pray. They employ a big vocabulary and seem to know all the right words. They are impressed with themselves and their prayer prowess. But God is not impressed with them.

Jesus said that when we pray to impress others, we do not pray with God's empowerment. When we pray insincerely, we already have our reward. The admiration of others is all we get. When we seek our own glory in prayer, we rob God of his glory and ourselves of our reward.

If you want to pray so God will hear and answer, be sincere. Don't say things you don't mean. And don't pray to impress someone else. After all, you're not talking to someone else; you're talking to God. God is impressed with sincerity, not vocabulary or volume.

Pray Secretly

Jesus continued, "But when you pray, go into your room, close the door and pray to your Father, who is unseen. Then your Father, who sees what is done in secret, will reward you" (Matt. 6:6). Pray secretly.

We need to make a distinction here. Nowhere in Scripture does God condemn public prayer. What Jesus said about the hypocrites was not to knock public prayer; it was to deter us from ostentatious prayer.

Public prayer, with God's blessing, is frequently exercised in the Bible. For example, when Solomon prayed at the dedication of the temple, he "stood before the altar of the LORD in front of the whole assembly of Israel" (2 Chron. 6:12). That's about as public as you can pray. Almost the entire ninth chapter of Nehemiah is a public prayer confessing Israel's sin. God loves to hear public prayer.

If public prayer touches the heart of God, why pray in secret? Because secret prayer equally touches the heart of God. God provides a secret pavilion for us. It's his secret place (Ps. 91:1), the place we can go when we need a secret island in a stormy world. It's the quiet place of prayer, the place of rest, near to the heart of God. Shutting the door on the outside world makes that secret place even more secret.

When I was in college, the dorm I lived in had a prayer closet, a tiny room on each floor for the guys to enter in secret and pray. I know that room was used at least twice a year—final exams in the fall and final exams in the spring.

When you purchase a house, you don't expect the multiple listing to read: "3 bedrooms, kitchen, living room, dining room, prayer closet, family room, full basement." Jesus was not talking about a special room, he was talking about shutting everything else out of your life when you talk to God.

That's exactly what we do when we close our eyes to pray. We enter our room and shut the door. We exclude everyone but God from our conversation. We pray in secret.

I find it helpful to have a place to pray, a special place I go to get away from the noise of the world. It's my treasured island. But sometimes it's not possible to take my journey to that special place. That's why God has equipped us with eyelids, to shut out the rest of the world while we pray in secret.

Follow the Leader. If Jesus says we should pray secretly, make sure you snatch some hours or minutes of the day to do just that. And when you are in the tumult of the crowd, you can still pray in secret by entering the room of your mind and shutting the doors of your eyes. Pray secretly.

Pray Sacredly

Furthermore Jesus instructed, "And when you pray, do not keep on babbling like pagans, for they think they will be heard because of their many words" (Matt. 6:7).

Praying pagans. Sounds like an oxymoron, doesn't it? When you pray, if you want God to hear you, don't pray as the pagans do. Instead pray sacredly. No vain repetitions.

When he said this, Jesus may have been thinking of the scribes, who "for a show make lengthy prayers" (Mark 12:40), or perhaps the priests of Baal who called on the name of Baal from morning until noon repeating, "O Baal, answer us!" (1 Kings 18:26).

Today we might think of the chants of the Hare Krishnas, the prayer-wheel of the Tibetan Buddhists, or the recital of the rosary. Jesus was teaching that prayer is not to be said with meaningless repetition. Prayer is a sacred conversation with God, a personal chat with a loving heavenly Father.

Aren't you glad you don't chant mantras when you pray? You don't use vain repetitions, right?

Don't be so sure.

Do you remember when you were just a little tyke, and your parents taught you to pray? At mealtime you folded your tiny hands and said, "God is great, God is good, and we thank him for our food." But when you were older, your parents may have said it was time for you to pray in your own words. No more "God is great, God is good"; you were on your own. What would you say? You stumbled at first, but then you said something like "Thank you, Lord, for this day and for this food. Bless it to our bodies. Amen." You expressed thanks in your own words.

Now be honest. How much have you varied those few words in twenty years, or even forty years? If you're still saying the same thing over and over, meal after meal, isn't that as much a vain repetition as the Pharisees prayed?

To pray sacredly means every time you pray you think about what you're saying. To pray sacredly means you abandon the "prayeraphrases" you may have adopted and begin to talk with God as a thankful child. To pray sacredly means you don't just rattle off a prayer, but you offer your prayer to the sovereign God.

Jesus taught his disciples to pray sacredly, with phrases new and fresh, phrases meaningful and reasoned. Don't pray yesterday's prayers. If God's mercies are new every morning, shouldn't our prayers be too?

PRAY SENSIBLY

About the pagans, Jesus said, "Do not be like them, for your Father knows what you need before you ask him" (Matt. 6:8). That means we should pray sensibly as well as sacredly. God is not unaware of our needs. On the contrary, he is fully informed of them, more than we are. We must be honest about our needs and resist the temptation to ask for things we don't need.

We can't fool God about a need that doesn't exist. We can fool our parents or children, sometimes even fool the church, but we cannot fool God. He knows exactly what we need even before we ask. As a father, I understood many of my children's needs better than they did. If I knew my children's needs when they were growing up, think how much more our loving heavenly Father knows our needs.

Jehovah said to Israel, "I am the LORD your God, who brought you up out of Egypt. Open wide your mouth and I will fill it" (Ps. 81:10). Fill it with what? With what the children of Israel needed. God better understood their needs than they did.

Remember, God has promised to supply all your needs, not all your greeds. Reflect a minute on your prayer life. When you pray, is it like reciting a Christmas list to Santa Claus? Do you send wish lists up to God hoping that in a weak moment he'll give in to one or two of your requests? That's not praying sensibly.

The door on little Fred's bedroom was ajar. His mother was walking down the hall past Fred's room when she heard her enterprising fifth-grader pray, "Lord, please make Boulder the capital of Colorado." This piqued his mother's interest so she listened quietly to the rest of Fred's prayer.

When he finished and climbed into bed, his mother went into the room. She sat on the edge of the bed and asked, "Fred, why did you pray that God would make Boulder the capital of Colorado?"

Fred explained, "Because that's what I put on my exam today!"

Too bad, Fred. God is not going to change the capital of Colorado to save your hide on an exam. That's not praying sensibly.

But we adults do the same thing. We pray that God will make us rich. We ask him for a red sports car. We intercede on behalf of our favorite football team. We pray that he will bless our sin. We ask him to protect us as we drive in excess of the speed limit. We don't always pray sensibly.

To fail to pray sensibly is to fail to pray with power. Jesus cautioned us that God has prior knowledge of our needs. In empowered prayer we match our petitions with God's omniscience. Anything less isn't prayer; it's fantasy.

PRAY SCRIPTURALLY

So how should we pray? That's what the disciples asked Jesus. That's what his disciples are still asking. We want to follow the Leader. We want to pray scripturally.

The prayer Jesus gave is our model. He said, "This, then, is how you should pray" (Matt. 6:9). Let's discover Jesus' pattern for empowered prayer.

The Lord's Prayer is divided in half between concentrating on God—which comes first—and concentrating on us, which naturally follows. In concentrating on God, Jesus focuses both on adoring God and petitioning him about things that relate to God. Later we are to petition for things that relate to us. There are seven petitions in all.

Concentrating on God

As with the other great prayers of the Bible, Jesus began with adoration to the Father. He addressed God as "Our Father in heaven."

It's evident this is a model for believers. Not everyone is privileged to address God as Father. There must first be a relationship with God.

Until we have trusted Jesus Christ as our Savior, we have no right to call God Father. It's our relationship with the Son that gives us a relationship with the Father. No wonder Jesus' model prayer began with adoration to the Father.

We approach God as a child approaches his father—full of love and confidence in his love for us. Paul even suggested we refer to God with the more intimate term *Abba*—Daddy.

Your relationship with your earthly father may be one you want to forget. Perhaps your father emotionally or sexually abused you as a child. It causes you pain every time you think about it. But Jesus reminds us that God is not our earthly father; he is our heavenly Father. There is no abuse or pain in your relationship with your heavenly Father. There is only love.

While we have an endearing relationship with him as a little child, we must not forget that our Father is the sovereign God of the universe. He deserves to be approached in the spirit of humble reverence. Too much chumminess with our heavenly Father destroys the impact of our relationship with him. Remember, God told his good friend "Do not come any closer" when Moses approached the consuming fire who is our God (Exod. 3:5). If you want to be empowered to pray, strike the proper balance between friendliness and fear. Show adoration for God before you ask things of him.

Petition One

Jesus' first petition relates to God, not to us. "Hallowed be your name."

When we hallow something, we hold it in reverence. We honor it. To hallow means to exalt. So to hallow God's name means to honor his person, to exalt him above all other beings.

In the ancient Near East a name was considered to be an expression of a person's nature. This was especially true of God. In the Old Testament God was called El. This name occurs in various combinations. For instance, El-Shaddai is the Almighty God. El-Elyon is the Most High God.

To pray that God's name be hallowed is to call the world to share your adoration of him. It's a way to invite the world outside the family of faith to exalt the Father by coming into the family in faith. This is the New Testament counterpart of the psalmist's call "Glorify the LORD with me; let us exalt his name together" (Ps. 34:3). Not a bad way to begin a prayer!

Petition Two

The second petition of this model prayer also relates to God. "Your kingdom come."

This is not a prayer for God to initiate his kingdom. His kingdom already exists. We see evidence of God's sovereign rule everywhere. The precision and majesty of the bodies of heaven. The regularity of the seasons. All are constant reminders of God's gracious rule.

God's kingdom on earth took a giant stride one night in the little town of Bethlehem. God was made flesh and dwelt among us. Later the Magi would ask, "Where is the one who has been born king of the Jews?" (Matt. 2:2).

But Jesus was not claiming his kingdom that silent night. He came as a babe to a stable, not as a regent to a throne. He came to die, not to rule. In fact, one day he ascended into heaven, leaving his kingdom behind.

So look around you. We live in God's kingdom. But if what you see is all there is, you have a right to be disappointed. That's why Jesus instructed us to pray, "Your kingdom come, your will be done on earth as it is in heaven." Isaac Watts wrote, "Jesus shall reign where'er the sun / Does its successive journeys run / His kingdom stretch from shore to shore / Till moons shall wax and wane no more."

Watts was clearly looking to a future day. Jesus shall reign—future tense. Now we pray for that day to come, but one day this petition will no longer be needed. The King will come in glory. At the sounding of the seventh trumpet, Revelation 11:15 says, "The kingdom of the world has become the kingdom of our Lord and of his Christ, and he will reign for ever and ever." What a day that will be!

But we aren't there yet. No flags have been unfurled, no trumpets blown. That's why Jesus told us to pray, "Your kingdom come." We must be faithful until the King returns, but pray for his soon return. That's not a bad way to continue a prayer.

Petition Three

The third petition in this pattern prayer is "Your will be done on earth as it is in heaven." This is the revealed will of God, the will that he expressed in his law.

Look around you. Turn on the evening news. Check out the *TV Guide*. It's pretty evident the will of God revealed in his law is not being done on earth today. We're to pray that it won't be long before it is.

We must make a critical distinction here. The decree of God is already in effect both in heaven and on earth. It's not subject to change by our prayers (Dan. 4:35; Eph. 1:11). No one can thwart the decree of God. But the will of God is not today being obeyed heartily, cheerfully, or completely here on earth. So it is the intense desire of everyone who hallows God's name that God's will one day will be obeyed completely on earth just as it's obeyed today in heaven.

I'm struck by two things about these petitions. First, their character. These are not stomach issues. They are not "how to make it through life" issues. They are much more important than that. They are eternal issues, issues of primacy. If we want to pray with power, our prayers should always address the eternal before they address the temporal.

Second, I'm amazed we are halfway through this model prayer, and we haven't yet mentioned ourselves. We have focused on adoring God and petitioning him for those things that relate to him.

Too often our prayers are only gimme prayers. You know the kind: gimme this and gimme that. We are the focus of our prayers. Often the third word in our prayers is me: "Lord, help me . . ." "Lord, show me . . ." "Lord, give me . . ." Me, me, me. We are the subject of too many of our prayers.

But in Jesus' pattern for prayer, God is the subject of prayer. He is the focus, not us. That's the way it should be. If we are to be empowered to pray, that's the way it must be.

Concentrating on Us

Even though Jesus first addressed the God issues as opposed to the stomach issues, he did not forget the stomach issues. He just put them in their proper place—secondary.

Having shown our respect to God, the scriptural way to pray is then to share our requests with God. It's now time to concentrate on us, and Jesus went hard to the hoop. He addressed man's most basic human need—food.

Petition Four

The Lord taught us to pray, "Give us today our daily bread" (Matt. 6:11). What did Jesus mean by today's bread? What is our daily bread?

So rare is this word that it's found only in the Lord's Prayer (here and in Luke 11:3). It makes a statement about the currency of our need. We need bread, and we need it right now. We ask God to provide it, for we need it, and we ask him to provide it in a timely manner.

Jesus did not want his disciples to worry about where their next meal would come from. The last verse of this sixth chapter relates to that. He does not want us to worry either. Instead he wants us to be empowered to pray. James says, "You do not have, because you do not ask God" (James 4:2). He wants us to trust him on a daily basis for our daily need.

The lessons are clear. We are to ask in faith. We are to ask in moderation. We are to ask in belief that God will provide. We ask for no more than we need. Each day we ask for no less.

Like many faith ministries, at Back to the Bible we ask God every day to provide for all our needs that day— spiritual, emotional, financial, physical.

I remember very distinctly several years ago when God blessed us with a $26,000 surplus at the end of our fiscal year, and we thanked him for meeting our financial needs that year. At the time our worldwide ministry needed an income of $55,000 a day to carry on God's work around the world. Our surplus meant we had operated 365 days and had enough left over for a half day more. That's living by faith and seeing God supply on a daily basis.

Petition Five

The fifth petition is for forgiveness. "Forgive us our debts, as we also have forgiven our debtors" (Matt. 6:12).

If we were forgiven at Calvary's cross, why do we need to ask God to forgive us now? Is there a daily need for forgiveness just as there is a daily need for bread? Absolutely.

The basis for our daily forgiveness is the once-for-all atonement secured by the blood of Christ at the cross. But we sin every day, and we need daily applications of that blood—not to save us again but to clean up the dirt of sin that continually soils our lives. According to 1 John 1:7, every time we genuinely confess the sin that creeps into our lives, God is faithful to forgive us of that sin by applying the blood of Christ to each day's sin.

But there's more. We the forgiven are to forgive others. "For if you forgive men when they sin against you," said Jesus, "your heavenly Father will also forgive you" (v. 14).

Do you want God to forgive your daily sin? Of course. But do you want him to forgive you to the same extent you forgive others? That's a different story. Jesus said God forgives us as we forgive others. In the very process of forgiving others, we are forgiven.

Clearly there is a relationship between prayer and forgiveness. But more to the point, there is a relationship between being empowered to pray and being empowered to forgive others. Empowerment in prayer comes from a right relationship with God and with others. So does forgiveness. No forgiveness from God, no empowerment. No forgiveness to others, no empowerment. It's just that simple!

Petition Six

The sixth petition of the Lord's Prayer is difficult, to say the least. "And lead us not into temptation." What does this mean?

Should we interpret temptation as mere testing? Was Jesus suggesting we should ask the Father not to test us? Unlikely. God tests us to make us stronger. This cannot be the meaning. Should we interpret temptation as seduction? Was Jesus suggesting we should ask the Father not to seduce us to sin? Definitely not. It would be totally contrary to God's nature to lead us to sin. "When tempted, no one should say, 'God is tempting me.' For God cannot be tempted by evil, nor does he tempt anyone" (James 1:13).

So what was Jesus saying? Perhaps he meant we should ask the Father not to allow us to enter situations where we could court sin.

An expanded paraphrase of this might be "Kind Father, seeing that we are so weak and prone to sin, please do not allow us to encounter those people or places today that will lead to our downfall. Help us to watch and pray so we don't fall into temptation. Our spirit wants to do the right thing, but our flesh is so weak" (see Matt. 26:41).

Essentially this is a confession of spiritual irresponsibility. It's an admission that we frequently take moral chances. We go places, watch things on television, hang out with people who place us in high risk of succumbing to temptation. It's the spiritual equivalent of going over Niagara Falls in a barrel. You're safer behind the railing on shore than in the barrel, even though you may survive the fall.

Spiritually mature people pray that God will order their steps to keep them from making wrong choices. We pray that God will keep us from the consequences of our own skewed logic and tarnished will. In short, we confess our weakness and ask God to steer us away from those people and places most likely to pounce on that weakness.

Is this petition important? If praying for daily bread is important physically, praying for spiritual strength and direction is no less important.

Petition Seven

And now the final petition of Jesus' pattern prayer. It's the twin to the preceding one. "But deliver us from the evil one."

The tempter is our ever-present foe. He is never far away. We dare not try to match wits with him. Satan is cunning, crafty, and just plain nasty. The wisest prayer we can pray with regard to Satan is that God will keep him away from us. That's precisely what Jesus was suggesting.

This is preventative prayer. It's like preventative maintenance or preventative medicine. I make it a daily habit to pray for my family. I do not pray that my son will be a powerful preacher or my daughters will be godly influences on the church and society. I'd like that, and that would be a good thing to pray. But that is less urgent than what I do pray daily: that God will protect them from the evil one.

For parents and grandparents, there is no greater privilege than praying for our children and granchildren. They are like precious jewels in our crowns of life. They need our prayers. Satan is out to destroy the family, and you and I possess a powerful weapon to defeat him. That weapon is prayer.

Remember how Job prayed for his family (Job 1:5) and even sacrificed for them in the event they were involved in secret sin? That's how you should pray for your family. Pray that God will bind the evil one. Pray that your family will be delivered from the deadly effects of drugs and alcohol and from godless friends and associates. Pray that they will find a meaningful place of service in a Bible-believing church. Don't think it is old fashioned to pray that your family be diverted from sin. Only Satan wants you to believe that.

When you bring your petitions to the Lord, pray the way Jesus did. Follow the Leader.

DOXOLOGY

The doxology "For thine is the kingdom, and the power, and the glory, for ever. Amen" is absent from some biblical manuscripts. If it wasn't part of the original prayer, it began surfacing early as part of it. The second century Didache version of Jesus' prayer features this doxology.

Some have conjectured that this doxology was borrowed from David's prayer in 1 Chronicles 29:11 and added to round out the Lord's Prayer liturgically. We won't know for sure until we ask the Lord himself.

If not a part of the Lord's Prayer, however, the doxology certainly is appropriate and adds a brilliant conclusion to a prayer designed as a pattern. It's the final peal of trumpets, the glorious conclusion to a prayer deeply concerned with adoring the Father.

Is the keen desire of your heart to pray with power? To be empowered to pray, we need insight into the proper way to pray. Who better to give that insight than the Lord Jesus. What has been called the Lord's Prayer is in reality a pattern for you and me. Concentrate on God first, then turn to yourself. Don't forget the physical in your petitions, but make the physical secondary to the spiritual. This is not just good advice; it's our Lord's command.

On-Line Prayer

The Lord's Prayer is beautiful, majestic, and awe inspiring. It's one of the outstanding pieces of literature in any language. So much so, a favorite spot of travelers to Jerusalem is the Pater Noster Church. At the "Our Father" Church the Lord's Prayer is inscribed on forty-four sets of tiles, each in a different language.

But Jesus did not give us this prayer to inspire us. It was not uttered to become great literature. He gave it as a pattern, a lesson in how to be empowered to pray. If we follow his pattern, we will plug into his power.

Our Father in heaven, hallowed be your name, your kingdom come, your will be done on earth as it is in heaven. Thank you, Father, for providing all we need—daily food, friends, even a schematic drawing to help us pray. We are not forgetful that we have sinned against you and others, and we ask your forgiveness. We promise to forgive others in the same way you have forgiven us. Guide our lives, Father, so we set nothing before our eyes that would cause us to sin or cause others to stumble. Keep Satan away from us and our family. We will reflect your power and your glory back to you, Father, because the glory belongs to you alone. Thank you for salvation through your Son, in whose name we thankfully pray. Amen.

Epilogue

The Bible is a book of prayers. I read somewhere that out of 667 prayers recorded in the Bible, there are 454 recorded answers. The persons we read about in the Bible obviously knew how to pray. They were empowered to pray. They got answers to their prayers.

I want answers to my prayers. So do you. I want to be empowered by God to pray. So do you. There is no better way to learn how to be empowered to pray than by soaking up everything we can from the great prayers of the Bible. We learn much more about praying from these great prayers than we do by reading dozens of books on prayer.

As I reflect on the ten great prayers of the Bible examined in this book, I reach five overarching conclusions about empowered prayer.

EMPOWERED PRAYER DOES NOT NEEDLESSLY PRAY IN THE DARK

Centuries ago land was power. The more land you owned, the more of a power baron you were. With the industrial revolution things changed. Suddenly money was power. It mattered less how much land you owned and more how much money you had. Things changed again with the information age. Now information is power. Just as sprawling acres gave way to bank accounts, both have given way to megabytes of data.

There's a spiritual application here. Information also is powerful in prayer. We should not needlessly pray in the dark. Being empowered to pray means being prepared to pray.

God will not turn a deaf ear to our thoughtless prayers. He'll answer us, even if we have made little preparation for prayer. But he gave us capable minds. God wants us to think through our prayers, to bring as much information as possible to prayer. God gave us the gift of intelligence; he obviously wants us to pray intelligently.

When my children were growing up, we had our family devotions together each night after supper. My wife and I still do. We have always read God's Word, interacted about what we read, and then spent some time in prayer. I wanted my children to be world Christians. So we kept a globe in our family room. Prayer cards from missionaries helped us picture their faces as we prayed for them. And we used Patrick Johnstone's helpful book *Operation World* to pray for a different country each night. We learned about the country's size, religious and ethnic makeup, and its current needs.

Praying with information is much more satisfying than praying, "Lord bless the missionaries." It's also much more pleasing to God. Don't pray in the dark when the light is at hand.

But empowered prayer requires much more than prepared minds. Our hands and hearts must be prepared as well. The psalmist said it best: "If I had cherished sin in my heart, the Lord would not have listened; but God has surely listened and heard my voice in prayer" (Ps. 66:18–19).

Spiritual preparation for prayer is just as necessary as mental preparation. We gather information to pray intelligently; we confess sin to pray effectively. When we prepare hearts and hands to pray, we concentrate on things that keep God from hearing us. We confess them as sin; we become "hearable." Confessed sin enables us to come to God with clean hands and a pure heart. It's the only way to come. We can only pray with passion when we pray with purity.

The sales representative gives an empowered presentation because he is prepared to sell. He has all the facts and figures at hand. He has thought through what he wants to say. He has put his heart into his presentation. He is empowered.

The athlete gives an empowered performance because she is prepared to run. She has trained, practiced, and done her warm-ups. She has mentally and physically prepared herself for this event. She is empowered.

Is prayer any different? If making a sale or winning a race is important enough to prepare for, doesn't prayer deserve the same?

Get the facts. Get yourself prepared. Get empowered.

EMPOWERED PRAYER REFLECTS ATTITUDES THAT PLEASE GOD

Success in prayer is largely dependent on the attitudes we bring to prayer. Hard attitudes mean hard praying. Right attitudes mean right praying.

My wife and I were sitting in the Red Carpet Room at the Los Angeles International Airport. We struck up a conversation with a woman seated across from us. She was Australian and on her way to Melbourne; we were headed for Sydney. I wanted to get some coffee, so I offered to get a cup for her as well. She declined, and I excused myself.

When I returned, I found the conversation had taken a turn for the worse. This otherwise pleasant woman was angry with the airline—and every airline. She complained about the food—it wasn't seasoned to her taste. She complained about the flight attendants—they were slow. She disliked the other passengers. The plane would take off late and arrive late. She didn't like the movie the airline was showing. She was going home to her family, but I suspected they weren't looking forward to her arrival.

Her flight was called a few minutes before ours. As she left I said, "I'll pray that you have a safe flight."

"I'll pray for you, too," she said.

As we flew across the Pacific, I definitely was not placing my trust for the safety of our fourteen-hour flight in the prayers of this woman. Her attitudes left me feeling sorry for her. God hears our attitudes when he hears our prayers. If we come to him with an attitude of complaint, pride, or bitterness, our prayers will be powerless.

God responds when we come to him with the attitude of the tax collector. This man was ashamed of his sin; he was humble; he felt unworthy for God to even hear his prayer. Still, he prayed. While he didn't have the right background, he did have the right attitude. That's how to be empowered to pray.

EMPOWERED PRAYER MAKES DEEP REQUESTS

We can talk to God about anything. It's one of the great privileges of the Christian life. Whatever our need, we can bring it to God in prayer. But what do we talk to him about? What do we most frequently request in prayer?

When we or others we know are sick, we pray for a speedy recovery. That's important. We pray that God will guide the surgeon's hands. We pray the church will have enough finances to complete its new family center. We pray God will give us success with our final exams. All these things are important.

These are the ABCs of prayer. They are the stuff of which most prayers consist. They are entry-level requests, common requests. But most of our prayers are too localized, relating to health, success, and money. God is much bigger than that. There's so much more to empowered prayer than entry-level requests. God wants us to crank up our requests to the next level.

John Newton wrote:

> Thou art coming to a King,
> Large petitions with thee bring;
> For his grace and power are such
> None can ever ask too much.

How do you know if your requests are too common? Keep a prayer diary. After you have prayed, write down what you prayed for. Record your daily prayer habits and requests. Make categories such as health, money issues, friends, church. Just as you would chart your fat or calorie intake, chart your prayer output.

If you keep a prayer journal consistently and honestly, I predict you'll be able to catalog the things you pray about on ten fingers, with a few fingers left over. Furthermore you'll see your requests mainly relate to health and finance issues. That's true with most of us because we don't think large enough or deep enough when we pray.

If we're to break out of the box and be empowered to pray, we have to pray some uncommon prayers. Add to the daily, temporal issues the larger issues of life, such as praying for forgiveness, for the power of God, and for the needs of others. To make a more exhaustive list you'll have to set aside some time to think about prayer before you pray. Don't be in such a hurry. Such thoughtfulness could mean the energizing power you're looking for in prayer.

Empowered prayer rises above the immediate, stretches beyond the temporal, and digs deeper than the mundane. Empowered prayer never runs out of things to pray for. It's prayer that grows with time and maturity. It develops as a spiritual skill. It moves off dead center and explores the uncharted waters of deeper things. The requests of empowered prayer not only deal with our needs but also reflect the agenda of God.

EMPOWERED PRAYER REFLECTS A RIGHT RELATIONSHIP WITH GOD

Paul once cautioned the Corinthians about Satan's efforts to outwit them, adding, "We are not unaware of his schemes" (2 Cor. 2:11). Being aware of the devil's devices is the first step in avoiding them.

One of those schemes relates to prayer. Satan attempts to distract us from prayer, to get us to debate inconsequential questions about prayer, to keep us from actually praying. If the devil can keep us talking about the appropriate position for prayer, the best place for prayer, or whether it's spiritual to write out our prayer, he'll keep us from praying.

The most important issue in prayer is our relationship with God. Do we know him as our Father? Have we trusted his Son, Jesus Christ, as our Savior? Is the Spirit of God dwelling in us, impelling us to pray? Is sin keeping us from close fellowship with the Father, Son, and Spirit? All these are relationship questions. They're the important issues in prayer.

Jesus had the best possible relationship with God the Father. He spoke only the words given to him by the Father. He did only the things commanded by the Father. Jesus knew the Father heard him when he prayed. When he asked for his friend Lazarus to be raised from the dead, Jesus said, "Father, I thank you that you have heard me. I knew that you always hear me" (John 11:41–42). There could have been no closer relationship. No sin stood between the Son and the Father.

But that's not always true with us. When we say or do things that displease God, when we live in the power of our own flesh instead of the power of his Holy Spirit, we put a damper on our prospects for effective prayer. That's why maintaining a right relationship with God is so vital to a vibrant prayer life. Make sure your relationship with God is all it can be, and you'll be empowered to pray.

Here's a final conclusion about being empowered to pray.

Empowered Prayer Receives Inspired Responses

Although relationship is the key to God hearing our prayers, it does not guarantee an affirmative response to them. Just because God loves us doesn't mean he always gives us what we ask. He didn't do that with his own Son; he won't with us either.

In an essay titled "The Efficacy of Prayer," C. S. Lewis wrote, "In Gethsemane the holiest of all petitioners prayed three times that a certain cup might pass from

Him. It did not. After that the idea that prayer is recommended to us as a sort of infallible gimmick may be dismissed."

Empowered prayer takes an empowered relationship. It means following an empowered pattern—the A-C-T-S formula. But even that does not make God a cosmic Santa Claus, granting our every wish. Our relationship with God is the basis for our prayers being heard, but it's also the basis for his response. God answers our prayers as he wills, not as we want. He is the Father, we are his children. God may not always answer as we wish, but thankfully his answers are always wiser than our requests.

Sometimes God answers yes, sometimes no, sometimes wait. These are not bad answers. No answer from God could be bad. They reveal the plan and program of God for your life.

You wouldn't know what that plan was if you hadn't asked. That's why being empowered to pray is so important. Empowered prayer reveals the mind of God. It shows you what God expects of you. It opens the doors for meaningful service to him.

One night a little girl surprised her mother when she concluded her prayer, "And now, God, what can I do for you?" I suspect God would like to hear that from us more often.

Vance Havner said the measure of any Christian is his or her prayer life. Being empowered to preach, to teach, to pastor a huge church pales in significance to being empowered to pray.

That power can be yours if you follow the example of the great prayers of the Bible. Pray with preparation. Pray with purity. Pray with pattern. Pray with power. But whatever you do, pray!

Alfred Lord Tennyson was right. "More things are wrought by prayer than this world dreams of." But perhaps he was only partially right. Dream of how many more things could be brought to pass with empowered prayer. God wants to give you that power. He wants you and me to pray with that power. And what's more, he has already made provision for that power.

Every Christian has the gift of God's Spirit to assist us in being empowered to pray. We have the examples of God's Word to teach us how to be empowered to pray. Now it's up to us. Follow the examples examined in this book. Glean every kernel of truth you can and then ask God to help you put them into practice in your prayer life. Being empowered to pray is an attainable goal. Others have obtained it, why not you?

Woodrow Kroll is general director of Back to the Bible in Lincoln, Nebraska, and Bible teacher on the *Back to the Bible* broadcast heard daily around the world.

Before assuming his responsibilities at Back to the Bible in 1990, Kroll spent more than twenty years training men and women for ministry at colleges and universities. He served ten years as president of Practical Bible College in Binghamton, New York. The author of dozens of books, he is a popular speaker at Bible conferences throughout the world.

Kroll received the M.Div. degree from Gordon-Conwell Theological Seminary, the Th.M. and Th.D. from Geneva-St. Alban's Theological College.

Woodrow and his wife, Linda, live in Lincoln, Nebraska.